KVETCH
and
ACAPULCO

Also by Steven Berkoff
WEST, LUNCH, and HARRY'S CHRISTMAS

KVETCH
and
ACAPULCO

Two plays by
STEVEN BERKOFF

GROVE PRESS
New York

Copyright © 1986 by Steven Berkoff

All rights reserved.

No part of this book may be reproduced, stored in a retrieval system, or transmitted in any form, by any means, including mechanical, electronic, photocopying, recording or otherwise, without prior written permission of the publisher.

All rights whatsoever in these plays are strictly reserved and applications for permission to perform them, etc., must be made in advance, before rehearsals begin, to Rosica Colin Ltd, I Clareville Grove Mews, London SW7 5AH

Published by Grove Press, Inc.
920 Broadway
New York, N.Y. 10010

Library of Congress Cataloging-in-Publication Data

Berkoff, Steven.
  Kvetch ; and, Acapulco.

  I. Berkoff, Steven. Acapulco. 1987. II. Title.
III. Title: Acapulco.
PR6052.E588K8 1987   822'.914   87-185
ISBN 0-802-10004-X
ISBN 0-802-13001-1 (pbk.)

Manufactured in the United States of America
First Edition 1987

10 9 8 7 6 5 4 3 2 1

KVETCH

An American Play About Anxiety

We all live under the shadow of the bomb – cancer – carcinogens – illness – unemployment – impotence – fear of fear – blacks – whites – police – rates – income tax – parking tickets – forgetting our lines – losing money – making too much money – losing hair – getting fat – getting ugly – being stupid – being unwitty – being shy – being foolish – worry about which stereo speakers – how to fix a car – a bike – learning the piano – fear of failing – not impressing – fear of others' strength – fear of weakness – fear of being exposed – not getting to work in time – not having a pension – security – old age – dying – war – injury in road accidents – fear of blindness – deafness – of not understanding the joke – fear of tough people – fear to take risks – fear to swim – to jump – to dive off a board – fear of disease – fear of moving – fear to sell – fear to buy – obsessional fear of spiders – dark cupboards – knives – muggers – fear of people – parties – crowds – clever people – fear of speaking your mind – fear of women – fear of men – fear of police – fear of anxiety – so this play is dedicated to the afraid.

CHARACTERS

FRANK
DONNA, Frank's wife
HAL, Frank's friend
MOTHER-IN-LAW, Frank's mother-in-law
GEORGE, a wholesaler Frank sells to

Note
Much of the speech is 'aside'. For simplicity, these passages are shown in italic.

The play was staged in front of a large painted wall depicting the freeways of Los Angeles as a surreal multi-laned jam of cars. There must have been about twenty lanes and one saw them all converge in the distance. Half-way up the wall was an impervious blue sky. Downstage was a table and four chairs around which the players performed.

The movement was generally sharp and dynamic. The declarations to the audience meant as confessions and given their full value. When a character was speaking his or her thoughts the action was frozen in the last position they were in and held for the duration, almost like a freeze-frame. For the scene in the bedroom we merely threw a giant bedspread on the table and, since the characters were already behind the table, they appeared with a little adjustment to be in bed. The piece of cloth used for the scene in the office became a tablecloth in the subsequent restaurant scene. Scenes should flow easily into each other much as a dissolve in a film.

A note from the author

Kvetch is a study of the effects of anxiety on the nagging kvetch that keeps you awake. It is the demon that wishes to taste your blood and sucks at your confidence. For many who can't live in the now, this is a real and terrible problem. We are beset by an array of problems that don't always sit and wait in the queue to be solved, but are liable at any instant to jump out of line and shout for your attention and kvetch you or kvetch at you until you have paid them some attention, even though in the meantime your present task may be ruined. They are the neglected children born of some distant anxiety. You may want them to go away and shout at them, confess them to shrinks or drown them at birth in drugs, but they will always return in some form or other. How often when we speak we have some background dialogue going on, sometimes to guide us and sometimes to protect us. Sometimes, though, the dialogue in the back of the head is truer than the one in the front. If only we could always speak the thoughts in the back; how much truer our communication would be. We are like icebergs slowly moving through life and seldom, if ever, showing and revealing what is underneath.

Kvetch was first performed on 15 March 1986 at the Odyssey Theater, Los Angeles, California. The cast was as follows:

FRANK	Kurt Fuller
DONNA	Laura Esterman
HAL	Mitch Kreindel
MOTHER-IN-LAW	Marcia Mohr
GEORGE	Ken Tigar
Director	Steven Berkoff
Producer	Ron Sossi
Set Designer	Don Llewellyn
Costume Designer	Ruth Brown

ACT I

SCENE I

DONNA: *I'm afraid . . . I'm afraid if he comes home late the cooking will be spoilt . . . I fear his wrath . . . not physically . . . but his scowling tongue . . . his looks . . . his moods. I get in a sweat. I know it's not my fault he is late, but I can't adjust . . . I can't be flexible and half cook it and then when he comes in finish it off. Have a glass of wine, darling – soon ready . . . I can't half do it – I think he'll be home and it won't be ready and he'll scowl and say . . .*

FRANK: For God's sake, I've been on the freeway for an hour then an hour back – I shlapp my guts out and you can't have a meal waiting at least . . . For God's sake, I've been on the freeway for an hour then an hour back – I shlapp my guts out and you can't have a meal waiting at least . . .

DONNA: *Sometimes he comes home even later and so I start the spinach on a small light . . . I keep the roast simmering – the potato latkes, that I can do on the spot. But if he's on time I rush around to get ready.*

FRANK: Can't you keep still, or at least prepare it, anticipate a bit . . . must you run around like a chicken with its head cut off . . . take it easy . . . other wives I know . . . you go in . . . 'Hello, darling,' they say to their husbands, 'have a Martini' . . . 'I brought a friend back,' he says. 'Sure, why not?' she replies easily and in a relaxed fashion . . . not phased out . . . plenty of food for a surprise guest . . . you sit . . .

DONNA: *If I prepare it too early I keep it in a dish over some boiling water and keep it hot but then he complains it's overcooked . . . it's mushy – the greens are soaking . . . it's like paste. I worry what to cook each night . . . I vary it – one night a roast – one night spaghetti – one night cauliflower au gratin and a salad . . .*

FRANK: The cauliflower's like a mush . . . it's like a milk shake . . . suppose I brought a friend home . . . for a surprise . . . since I want to be a mensch sometimes and say, 'Hal, do yourself a favour . . . Coupla beers, Charley . . . Come home

1

to my place – why should you go home to an empty apartment? . . . what life is that? Nu? You go home and who welcomes you . . . the cat? So come for a nosh . . . Listen, gorden blurr it's not . . . you know what I'm saying . . . we'll have a homely meal and put our feet up and watch a movie . . . sure we got cable . . . have a beer . . .'

MOTHER-IN-LAW: You're buying cheap oil, it burns the latkes.

DONNA: Ma, I use the same oil you use.

HAL: You sure it'll be OK?

FRANK: Of course I'm sure . . . I'm positive . . . I'd like you to . . . why not? . . . you'd like her . . . it'll make a change . . . a new face spices the evening . . . we'll exchange kvetches . . . I mean stories about our anxieties . . . ha! . . . ha! . . . then we'll watch Paul Newman killing a few people . . . wadya say? . . . *Oh God . . . I hope he says no . . . I don't know what we'll talk about . . .*

MOTHER-IN-LAW: A little pepper goes a long way . . .

DONNA: Ma!

FRANK: *Suppose the bitch hasn't enough food . . . suppose she has overcooked it 'cause we're late . . . or even worse gone to bed because her ulcers are playing up . . . Gavolt or shit . . . or maybe her mother's there who belches . . . Of course it's Friday . . . her fucking mother will be there belching and the food will be overcooked and I smell the stinking cabbage twenty floors down . . .*

HAL: You sure you want me to come?

FRANK: Look I'm not forcing you . . . you're your own man so make it another night . . . when you're free . . . you say, 'Frank . . . how's tonight?' We don't stand on ceremony . . . any time . . . our house is an open door . . . you say the day . . . next week . . . next month . . . when you like . . . if it's not convenient tonight . . .

HAL: Well . . . hell, why not? . . . You're right, you know since Betty left I must say I hate to go home . . . I hate it, you're right . . . an empty place . . . the breakfast dishes still there from last week . . . Are you sure your wife will have enough?

FRANK: Look . . . when she buys she doesn't buy for one – like a shrivelled-faced vstinkiner that maybe asks for scraps for the cat . . . for a regiment she buys. You open the fridge . . . you can't shut it . . . Have enough!! When she shops at Vons the shares go up!

MOTHER-IN-LAW: You shouldn't be so stingy with the garlic!

DONNA: Ma, it's enough.

FRANK: But listen, don't come for us . . . don't put yourself out just because I asked . . . I won't be offended . . . you do what you want . . . listen, who makes a deal out of it? . . . I sense a certain reluctance . . . when you *really want* to come . . . you say . . .

HAL: You mean we should make it another night?

FRANK: Hell, no! Tonight is great . . . you're welcome . . . my life, it makes no difference . . . every night's the same . . .

HAL: OK, I'll come.

FRANK: *Oh shit!* . . . good!

HAL: *I don't know . . . should I go there? . . . At home it's quiet and I know who I am! What I am . . . why should I sit with them . . . what can I say? I'll choke up . . . they'll find me boring . . . He's happily married . . . two kids . . . I'm forty . . . separated . . . can't hold a wife . . . living alone like a monk with a cat, and I should watch them with their kids . . . warm laughter, gaiety . . . fulfilling hours . . . growth . . . struggle . . . achievement . . .*

MOTHER-IN-LAW: You bought such skimpy chops, will it be enough?

HAL: *I'll sit there and feel like a lump . . . like a leech on society . . . incomplete . . . fruitless . . . dull. I'll choke . . . she'll ask me what I do at nights . . .*

DONNA: Oh God, the latkes are burnt . . .

MOTHER-IN-LAW: I told you, cheap oil.

HAL: *What do I do? . . . Sit and watch TV . . . sit in the local bar . . . visit a hooker . . . or sit in with Ma . . . What do I do, she'll ask me . . . Oh God! . . .*

(DONNA sets out plates and forks, and mimes serving pie. FRANK and HAL switch pieces. DONNA switches them back.)

DONNA: I'm sorry if it was a bit overcooked . . . I was expecting you earlier . . . I had it perfect . . . it was just right . . . I expected you by seven o'clock and by seven-thirty I put it on the light . . .

FRANK: *Oh, for God's sake shut that stupid hole.*
DONNA: Next time call and tell me you're bringing home a friend and I would have gotten more chops from Vons . . .
FRANK: But darling, I did call . . .
DONNA: Call earlier . . .
FRANK: What, I have to call in April for a dinner in May?
(DONNA and HAL speak fast, overlapping.)
DONNA: Have some more, Hal.
HAL: I've had plenty really.
DONNA: You sure?
HAL: I'm full.
DONNA: You sure now?
HAL: Couldn't eat another thing.
DONNA: Just a tiny bit more?
HAL: No thanks, it was great.
DONNA: You sure?
HAL: I had plenty . . . really . . .
MOTHER-IN-LAW: He's got a mouth . . . if he was hungry, he'd open it.
FRANK: *Don't embarrass me . . . I'm sweating in shame . . . Oh God!*
(MOTHER-IN-LAW belches.)
Oh God, may the earth open up . . . may a bomb drop on this house!
(Pause. Eating sounds.)
DONNA: You know my husband is so unpredictable . . . he says one thing and does another . . . lives for his work . . . so can you get a straight answer when he'll come home . . . if he can take another order he will . . .
MOTHER-IN-LAW: He wants to look after his family . . . a wonderful worker . . . and a wonderful son-in-law . . . a great provider . . . what more can you ask? . . . Listen . . . they won't starve . . . that you can assure yourself of . . . my life, he's a jewel . . . you know what I'm saying, what's-your-name . . . Hal?
HAL: Yeah . . .
MOTHER-IN-LAW: Yeah, Hal . . . he's a provider . . . like you won't see him drinking it away in a bar, God forbid . . . like

those bums at the end of the road . . . gavolt, you can hear them . . . You don't drink, do you . . . er, Hal?
HAL: Er, not too much . . . you know sometimes . . . with a friend . . . Christmas ha! ha! . . . but not much . . . no . . . don't like to lose control . . . glass of wine . . . maybe . . . you know with a meal . . .
MOTHER-IN-LAW: He's the jewel of my life, they don't come better.
(MOTHER-IN-LAW belches.)
FRANK: *I wish they were dead. Both of them. I married the mouth and inherited the belch. Could I have done better, I ask myself. I'd like to leave . . . I haven't got the guts . . . I swear I could leave right now . . . yes, right this minute, I could scream and jump out of the window . . . closed or not . . . go screaming down the street . . . me screaming and running shouting . . . fuck fuck fuck fuck fuck . . . shit and fuck . . . you stupid fucking belching cunt . . . shut up . . . but I can't . . . I sweat and squirm instead.*
(HAL and DONNA – improvised overlap:)
DONNA: Are you sure you're not hungry? There's more pie, I know it was scorched, let me get you some . . .
HAL: (With DONNA) I'm fine, really . . . no, thank you, I couldn't eat another thing, really . . . I'm stuffed . . . thank you . . . Can't eat another bite . . .
DONNA: *He's scowling at me . . . he's ashamed of me. I do what I can but I'm afraid all the time . . . What must his friend think? . . . The dinner was ruined but the apple pie was nice . . . with cream that was nice . . . I've got a stomach ache . . . my ulcer's killing me . . . I want to go to the bathroom and mix some Milk of Magnesia but I'm afraid to go . . . in case it looks funny . . . My make-up is runny . . . His friend must think I'm stupid . . . he looks so intelligent . . . Why didn't Frank phone? . . . Just a quick call to warn me . . . Am I sweating? . . . What shall I say now?* . . . Now that you're separated, Hal . . . what do you find to do at nights? . . .
HAL: Oh God . . . at nights . . . well . . . I . . . *Sit indoors and cry . . . smoke myself to death . . . pick my nose . . . watch TV till I fall asleep with a bottle of Scotch . . . count the hairs on the comb*

when I go into the bathroom . . . ring a call girl . . . or jerk off in front of my favourite centrefold spread . . . pace up and down . . . fall asleep and wait for the morning so that I can do something . . . scream or take Valium . . . think about overdosing . . . at nights . . . well . . .

FRANK: *What a stupid question to have asked a man who's separated . . . what a stupid question to ask him. Now what does she think he does . . . throw dinner parties for movie stars?*

MOTHER-IN-LAW: *That's a question to ask a single man . . . yech!*

HAL: At nights . . . well . . . *I don't know what to say . . . I feel sick . . . Look at them . . . they don't have to do anything at night. They sit and enjoy each other . . . have a dinner together . . . talk about the day . . . comfort each other . . . read and be silent in each other's support . . . lean on each other . . . What can I do? At nights . . . they go home and there's a light on . . . a golden light that attracts you like a moth to the warmth . . . at nights . . . well . . .*

FRANK: *I wish I'd never asked him . . . I should have shut my mouth . . . I want to be like other men with families . . . be a mensch . . . friends pop in . . . always something on the stove . . . play a game of rummy . . . tell jokes . . . have my wife cook something succulent . . . be witty . . . make them laugh . . . I wish I could tell a joke . . . I must know one . . . now what joke can I tell? . . . But suppose it falls flat . . . suppose I forget the tag line . . . suppose they look or feel embarrassed . . . but one has to try . . . do it . . . go for it . . . What's the worst that can happen? . . . You won't die . . . break the ice . . . be a bit bold . . .* Have I told you . . .

HAL: What I do at nights . . . sorry . . . you were saying . . .

FRANK: No, no, sorry, go on . . . I interrupted *you* . . . please . . .

HAL: Sure I can wait . . .

DONNA: Honey, he was just telling us what he does . . .

HAL: At nights!

DONNA: Yes, at nights . . .

(MOTHER-IN-LAW belches.)

FRANK: Oh, Ma, for God's sake!

DONNA: She can't help it . . . don't be so unkind, Frank, she's an old lady . . . don't be so mean . . . I'm sorry, Hal . . .

HAL: No, really, not at all, I don't mind . . .
DONNA: She's a sick old lady, Frank, but she's got spirit . . . she's just getting on a bit . . . Hal understands, Frank . . . you got to make allowances for older people . . . you'll be old one day, Frank, and I hope our kids are more understanding than you . . .
FRANK: *This is beautiful, what an evening . . . So tomorrow it will be all over the warehouse of Frank's crazy family . . . I feel sick . . . my food wants to come up or go down and miss out the middle man* . . . I just said, 'For God's sake' – so what does that make me, Hitler? I said, kill her, didn't I . . . gas her . . . send her to the chambers. So kill me . . . What did I say, Hal, that was such an unexcusable sin? . . . Are older people some kind of saints . . . we should hold our breath while she belches and farts? . . .
DONNA: She doesn't fart . . . For God's sake, Frank, don't be so insidious . . .
MOTHER-IN-LAW: *I'm an old lady . . . soon I'll die . . . good riddance and feh! A fine pair . . . do you think I care? . . . I'm finished . . . Give me a good book and a meal a day, or they can send me to a home. I know they want to send me to a home . . . but it's cheaper to keep me in a two-roomed pen and hire a housekeeper for a couple of hours a day . . . and once a week, big deal, I come here . . . I tell you I don't come here for the food. I come here 'cause I'm sick of the four walls. Look at them. She's become a drudge. So all she could get was him . . . worry guts. Works all his life and hasn't a pot to piss in. Still that's all she could get at thirty . . . the dregs . . .* Take no notice, Donna, I'm going to bed . . .
HAL: Well, at nights . . . I get home and you know . . . I uh find plenty to do . . . you'd be surprised . . . how one finds . . . so much . . . that was, er, left undone . . . yeah, you know . . . letters . . . that weren't written . . . yeah, friends you neglected . . .
FRANK: *I bet he fucks a lot, dirty bastard . . . living alone . . . lucky single fucker . . .*
HAL: And reopen . . . those old friendships . . . check out the old pals, like people you'd forgotten . . . I kind of got involved

in my marriage and didn't see the old faces . . . you know how it is . . . and now I'm single again . . .

FRANK: *Single . . . even the word tastes dirty . . .*

HAL: . . . like single again . . . I thought, hey, why not look up the old pals . . . you know, get out have a drink . . . maybe a reunion . . .

DONNA: *Friends . . . lucky man . . . seeing people . . . new people . . . friends . . . I'm so hungry for friends I can almost taste the word on my lips . . . we never see anyone . . . I hate being married to him . . . to see his miserable complaining face every day . . . I want to run away . . . I could leave tomorrow . . . if I had the guts I would . . . leave the kids and him . . . never see anyone . . . just him and his guts to fill and the inside of a supermarket three times a week . . .*

HAL: Not that marriage isn't wonderful . . . I mean it's good . . .

FRANK: *Yeah, like a pile on your anus . . .*

HAL: But it never gave me time to explore . . . and visit old friends . . . you know . . . re-acquaint yourself with the old . . .

FRANK: Frenz!

HAL: You're right, Frank, sure I miss her but then you've got to fill the gap with . . .

FRANK: *Frenz!! . . .* Friends . . . yeah, I know . . .

HAL: That's it . . . like I had a pal . . . this friend from work . . . and, hell, when he left I kind of lost touch . . . like, you know, so anyway one day I was cleaning my apartment . . .

DONNA: Ah! You have no one to clean for you? . . .

HAL: No . . . I don't . . .

DONNA: *I clean every day . . . I clean and scrub and launder and wash up for the ungrateful bastard who won't even fuck me any more . . . I would clean for him, poor guy . . . I wonder if he's circumcised?*

HAL: Yep, I clean for myself, I'm a regular housewife now . . . hahahahaha . . . now I know how she felt . . . hahahahaha!

DONNA: *He has a really sweet laugh and is a nice person . . . The evening is taking a turn for the better and during this laughter I am going to sneak out for some Milk of Magnesia 'cause my ulcer's killing me and if I go out boldly now – no one will notice . . .*

FRANK: Regular housewife . . . hahahahahahahahahahahaha-hahaha! *God! The evening's taking off. I'm not sweating so much and my stomach isn't in knots . . . although I badly want to shit, but I'm afraid to now while we're just getting going, I'll get the belcher to bed and then I'll tell my joke* . . . How you doing, Ma? (MOTHER-IN-LAW has fallen asleep.) You OK? How was the food? . . . Good to see you . . . Isn't she sweet? . . . *Get rid of her . . . if I crap now it'll leave him with them and then they'll go silent and get uncomfortable . . . I'll tell a joke and then put on the TV . . . Shit, where'd she go?* . . . Donna? Are you doing the coffee, darling? . . .

DONNA: (Muffled from the next room) No! Do you want some?

FRANK: What are you doing, honey? . . .

(Silence.)

Are you OK? . . .

DONNA: Hmmmmmmmmmm!

FRANK: Regular housewife, huh! Hahahahahahahahaha! Come in, honey . . . *Oh fuck and shit, come in, you idiot, while we're having a good time . . . don't leave me to hold the fort alone* . . . Honeeeey?

DONNA: Sorry, folks . . . just powdering my nose . . . haw haw . . .

(DONNA appears with white all over her lips.)

FRANK: *My God!*

HAL: *Hahahahahahaha!*

FRANK: *My God!*

DONNA: You want some coffee, everybody? . . . *What are they staring at? Do I look funny?* . . . Sorry, Hal, you were just saying what you do at nights . . .

HAL: Yes . . . yes . . . sorry . . . no . . .

(FRANK gestures to DONNA to wipe her lips. DONNA does.)

I was just saying about nights . . . yes . . . you know one night is much like another on the whole and I was cleaning up my room when I came across this old diary . . . you know, with the telephone numbers in the front, so I called up this old friend . . . I hadn't seen him for at least twenty years it had to be . . . from school I knew him . . .

DONNA: *I hated school.*

FRANK: *He's boring me to death . . .*
MOTHER-IN-LAW: *I think I've got a bowel movement coming on, maybe a fart will release the pressure . . .*
HAL: Yeah, twenty years at least . . . let's see . . . I last saw him . . . in 1960 . . . yeah . . . it would be that . . .
FRANK: *I'll tell a joke . . . I've got to speak . . . say something . . . anything . . . I never say anything . . . Once the party gets going I say less and less and everyone else takes over . . . Look at him talking away . . . He's getting warmed up.*
HAL: . . . and so I called and said, 'Hello . . . can I speak to Bob Lipinski? . . .
DONNA: A Pole?
HAL: Yes . . . that's right . . .
DONNA: I knew a Pole called Lipinski, from work.
HAL: You're kidding . . .
DONNA: Nope, the same name anyways . . .
MOTHER-IN-LAW: *I love Polish pickle . . .*
FRANK: *Now how does that joke go? . . .*
DONNA: Yeah, he had red hair and tons of freckles . . . and he had a bulbous nose . . . like an onion at the end . . . and he had a small gap in his teeth . . . so he had a lithp . . .
FRANK: *How come she knew him so well? . . . She never told me . . .*
MOTHER-IN-LAW: *Polish herrings are nice . . .*
DONNA: And when he spoke, he lithp . . . like that . . . 'Good morningth . . . How are you, Thylvia? . . .'
HAL: Thylvia? . . .
DONNA: Well, my middle name is Sylvia and I went through a phase of *hating* Donna . . .
HAL: Sylvia's a very pretty name . . . mind you, I like Donna . . .
DONNA: Everybody was called Donna at school but now I don't know anybody called Donna . . .
HAL: Donna is more unusual, I think . . . it's got a kind of feel to it . . .
DONNA: What do you prefer? . . . I mean, if you had a choice? . . .
HAL: Hell, I like both . . . but Donna is definitely more unusual . . . you don't hear that name so often . . .

DONNA: Yeah, Sylvia's a bit common . . .
HAL: Oh, no . . . it's a good name . . . I like both but Donna is more . . . you.
DONNA: You think? . . .
MOTHER-IN-LAW: I nearly called her Barbara!
DONNA: Help! Barbara . . . can you imagine . . . at school . . . Babs! . . . Yukky!
HAL: Do you know . . . I have a middle name . . . yep . . . I have one.
DONNA: Oh, tell us!
HAL: Ooooh, you promise to forget it immediately after I tell you . . .
DONNA: It can't be that bad . . . not as bad as Babs! Yukky!
HAL: It's so awful . . . I can barely bring myself to say it . .
DONNA: Go on . . . go on!!!
HAL: Promise not to laugh.
DONNA: Promise . . .
FRANK: *I promise not to throw up* . . .
HAL: OK, here goes . . .
DONNA: Oh, go on, he's teasing us now . . . you should worry . . . do you know what Frank's middle name is? . . .
FRANK: *What . . . is she fucking crazy? . . . What's the matter with you? . . . Idiot* . . .
HAL: Come on, Frank . . . give up the goods . . . what else do they call you? You should know what they call him at work . . .
DONNA: Why, what do they call him?
FRANK: Aw, come on, Hal . . . *Give us a break, you prick* . . .
HAL: Can I say, Frank? . . . I thought you would have told them . . .
FRANK: You know how it is . . . we all give each other names . . . it's a joke at work . . .
DONNA: So what do they call you? . . . What do they call you? . . .
HAL: Can I say, Frank . . . huh, can I tell them?
FRANK: *You stupid jerk . . . I'm sorry I ever asked you . . . You should rot next time in hell before I offer you my home* . . . Yeah, go on . . . it's no big deal . . .

HAL: Well, they call him . . .
DONNA: Go on, go on . . .
HAL: The Kvetch!!!!
(ALL laugh.)
FRANK: *Stop having such a good time at my expense!! I haven't spoken in hours . . . I've got to say something . . . my joke! Let me see if I remember it . . . Ah yes . . . haw haw haw haw haw haw haw . . . I hope to God I don't fuck it up. Maybe I should practise it in my head first . . . No, I'll just come out with it . . .* Hey, Hal . . . listen, have you heard the one about . . . (Sniffs the air, smelling MOTHER-IN-LAW's fart.) Pooh! What's that? You haven't left the gas on, have you, Donna . . . ?
DONNA: No . . . oh! . . . Oh, dear . . . maybe I did . . .
FRANK: Christ, I think you must have . . . Oh no! . . . I told you, Donna, we must get rid of that old stove . . . it's a worn-out useless piece of junk . . . it stinks . . . so let's get rid of it!!!!! . . .
MOTHER-IN-LAW: Well, I think I'm going to bed soon . . .
HAL: Heard the one about what, Frank? . . . *God I went down well . . . I found my voice . . . it's wonderful . . . I was speaking without choking or coughing . . . without stammering or flushing . . . but clearly amusing . . . I must be making an improvement . . . this is good. I am not sweating or worrying . . . yet . . . Oh, God, I shouldn't have said that, something is bound to bother me . . . I know it will . . . any second . . . I was having too good a time . . .*
FRANK: Oh, yes . . . oh, it's nothing . . . just a joke . . .
HAL: Aw, come on, Frank . . .
DONNA: Yes . . . go on, Frank . . . tell us . . . *He's not told a joke in years . . . I have never known this to happen before . . . This is amazing . . . because you have to remember a joke . . . you have to take risks . . . you might not get the punch line right and then you will be left with egg dripping down your face, and he is actually daring to say one . . . It's giving . . . it's risking . . . it's baring yourself and he never does that . . . This must be costing him . . . I bet I'll have a heavy wash day tomorrow.*
FRANK: No, it's nothing . . . what was it . . . a shtick . . . a piece of nothing . . . a soupçon . . . what? . . . just a gag I heard at

work. . . . *Oh, fuck and shitass, don't make me say the bastard thing now . . . I can't remember, fuck it, or maybe I can . . . The stink is still awful . . . yukk! Wish I could shoot her . . . sometimes if I had a knife . . .* (Mimes stabbing MOTHER-IN-LAW violently.) *Horror horror horror horror . . . Oh, I feel a bit better . . . Fuck it, I'll tell the fucking joke . . .* So, there was an . . .

DONNA: Darling, darling . . . what's a soupçon? . . .

FRANK: Who knows these things? . . . You hear a saying and it sounds right . . . I forget . . . I knew but I forget but I know that I use it right but I forget what it is.

DONNA: How can you use it right then if you forget?

MOTHER-IN-LAW: *She's right . . . when she's right she's right!*

FRANK: You sense it . . . the feeling is right although the origin may be lost . . . *What's the matter with her? . . . She's fucking crazy . . . she's contradicting me with her mouth in public, already. When she don't know from nothing, the ignoramus slut, but hold her hand out for money, that she knows.*

MOTHER-IN-LAW: Who wants coffee, who wants tea? . . . (ALL begin overlap improvisation about the coffee.) Coffee?

HAL: Yeah . . .

MOTHER-IN-LAW: Coffee?

FRANK: Yeah . . .

MOTHER-IN-LAW: Tea?

DONNA: Coffee . . .

MOTHER-IN-LAW: Sugar? Sugar?

HAL: No . . .

FRANK: One sugar in mine . . .

DONNA: Honey, you don't need sugar . . .

FRANK: I can have sugar . . . OK, half a sugar . . .

MOTHER-IN-LAW: Milk?

HAL: Do you have any non-dairy creamer . . . ?

MOTHER-IN-LAW: No, we don't . . .

FRANK: Yeah, we do . . . we've got Mocha Mix . . .

DONNA: No, we don't . . .

FRANK: Yeah, we do . . . it's in the fridge behind the bicarb . . .

DONNA: No, I froze it . . .

FRANK: You froze the Mocha Mix?!!!
HAL: That's OK, I'll just have some milk in my soupçon . . . haw haw haw haw . . .
(End of overlap improvisation.)
MOTHER-IN-LAW: *They bring me here once a week and I'm shlepping trays . . . Next they'll want me to scrub the floors . . .*
HAL: *I am having a wonderful time . . .*
DONNA: *The dinner party is going so well and I'm so proud . . . Haw haw haw haw . . .*
FRANK: *You two fucking hyena idiots . . . sitting in your stinking mother's fart . . . I feel uncomfortable and my mouth is dry but let's get the bastard thing over with . . .* Well, there was an Englishman, an Irishman and a Jew . . .
DONNA: Haw haw haw haw haw haw haw . . .
HAL: *This is really a nice family . . . warm-hearted . . . kind . . . How nice of him to ask me . . . See, I'm warming up . . . I feel OK again . . . Maybe one day I'll have them over to me . . . Yeah, I'll make dinner for them . . . but I'm not a good cook . . . Oh, no, I've got the demons coming on . . . go away, go away!! I was happy before . . . Go away! . . . I can't be invited here again and not reciprocate . . . They maybe don't expect it but how many times can I be invited before reciprocating? Once . . . twice . . . three times? . . . I could make something simple and we'll have a few drinks . . . We'll eat in the kitchen and then go in the living room for coffee . . . Must I think of it now? . . . I'll make some snacks . . . just a little soupçon of everything . . . I'll get it from the deli and then we'll have it in the living room . . . Should we start in the living room with drinks then go to the kitchen? . . . But if I'm preparing something hot, say a soup, I'll have to leave them in the living room with a drink and run in and out . . . or . . . why not start off in the kitchen with drinks? . . . But then the stereo is in the living room . . . Oh, shit . . . we can play some music and have a few drinks and then go in the kitchen . . . or still better . . . I'll leave them with a drink and bring the stuff into the living room . . . But why shlapp it in the living room when the kitchen is supposed to be where you dine? . . . Unless I bring the stereo into the kitchen . . . but what if we go after to the living room for coffee? . . . I can't shlapp it back*

again ... Maybe I'll buy another cassette deck ... No, I'll put all the stuff in the living room and run in and out and most of the stuff will be cold anyway, except for the soup and the coffee ... Mind you, it's cosy in the kitchen ... There's a big wooden table in there ... In the living room there's small tables so I'll have to take the salad round ... to where people are sitting at the small tables ... There's no centre table so we couldn't all face each other with a bottle in the middle ... I'll have to walk around with the bottle ... but at least there'll be space ... but it won't be so warm as the kitchen ... Oh, fuck it, we'll eat in there ... that's fine ... take the consequences ... But it would be nice for them to see the living room ... after, with coffee ... not before ... no after ... not before? Wait! ... We could eat in the living room if I brought the table into the centre, then I could put the bottle in the middle ... That means taking the table from the kitchen ... but then after we've eaten we'll have to sit in the living room with all the dirty dishes or make a fuss clearing them up whereas in the kitchen you just leave it all and say, let's stretch our feet in the living room ... No, I know what to do ... I'll kill myself instead ... then I won't have to do anything ... take an overdose or get run down by a truck ... This is why God breathed life into me ... to decide whether the table goes in the living room or in the kitchen ... oooohh!

FRANK: So there was an Englishman, an Irishman and a Jew ... Ah, they're smiling ... like I hope we'll enjoy ourselves ... And they meet in a bar ...

DONNA: You know Jews don't go to bars ...

FRANK: I have never been to a bar!? Eh! You have never seen me in a bar?

DONNA: Yeah, but you're not a real Jew ...

FRANK: What?

DONNA: No, no, I mean, not like those Jews ... er ... real ones like ... Oh, shit, why does he embarrass me? ... He knows what I mean ... he knows I mean the Jews like his father who wear a hat in the house and dandruff over their coats and smell of onions, yellow flaccid ones with round backs and beards ... You know, like Orthodox ...

FRANK: Listen to her, Hal . . . like a Jew can't be seen in a bar . . . What do you think, they can't mix a bit? . . . You think all Gentiles are uncircumcised anti-Semitic yid-kicking bastards . . . where the kitchen stinks of grease and they never wash their hands after going to the toilet? . . . What, you carry that old legend that the goy just drink till they vomit and at weddings you're lucky to get a hamburger and a can of beer? . . . No . . . you're wrong . . . some of my best friends are goyim . . . very decent people . . . 'cause they don't shtipp lox down their guts on Sunday until it comes out of their ears and have stomach ulcers it doesn't mean they're bad . . . so I'll carry on . . . *I've found my voice again . . . Hal is quiet with a new-found respect for my acid humour and the party is not so bad . . . Wonderful, I've got the floor and no kvetch . . . I'll tell the joke . . . this is wonderful . . .* So they were in a bar and the Englishman says drunkenly . . . 'I've been mistaken for some very important people in my time . . . You know, once I was taken for Winston Churchill' . . . and then the Irishman says . . . 'Oh, that's not such a big deal, you know, once I was walking down Dublin High Street and a woman come up to me, "Holy Father, if it's not the Pope himself" . . . and the Jew says . . . 'That's nothing . . . well, I was sitting in a movie house and the picture was so wonderful I thought why not see it again . . .'

DONNA: Hahahahahahahahahahaha!

FRANK: Wait a minute . . . I ain't finished yet . . .

MOTHER-IN-LAW: Here's the coffee . . .

DONNA: Shush, Ma . . . he's telling a joke . . . just a minute . . . he's nearly finished . . .

HAL: Come on, Frank . . . go on . . . 'Vy not,' he says . . . vy not indeed . . . haw haw haw haw haw haw haw haw!

FRANK: So he's sitting in the movie house and thinks, 'So vy not see it again' . . . *Gosh, this is going really well . . . I'm excited . . . Hey, I can easily hold them there in the palm of my hand . . . I knew I could do it, so why do I hold back, why lack confidence when I'm such a marvellous story-teller? . . . I have the power . . . I know I do . . . but I always let the others do it . . . let them be funny . . . take the stage . . . impress the ladies*

and I go quiet and choke and then I open my mouth with a
prepared speech and it sounds like death 'cause it didn't come out
when it went in my head . . . I let it spoil and then when I let it
out it stinks like day-old herring you forgot to put back in the
fridge . . . Oh, God, the joke's a prepared speech so what am I
talking about? Yeah, but it's different, you got to use timing.
Now timing's the gold of the comic . . . without timing, a shitty
story will come across like a shitty story. But with timing a shitty
story will sound like poetry . . . no, not poetry . . . but like
amazing . . . like brilliant . . . A golden observation . . . but a
brilliant observation will sound like drek in the mouth of a
shmock! You know . . . don't laugh, but maybe I could do
cabaret . . . Yeah, get up on volunteer nights in the bar down the
street . . . 'Hey, ladies and gentlemen, what's a Jewish
American princess's favourite wine?' . . . Gentiles love Jewish
jokes . . . I could get up and tell a lot of anti-Semitic jokes and I
could get away with it . . . Oh, I know a beauty . . . I'll save it
for after this . . . Yeah, vy not indeed . . . so he sees the film
again, he likes it so much that he stays for the last show . . .
Why are they yawning? . . . No, it's not going down too well
. . . it's terrible . . . I promise God I won't tell anti-Semitic jokes
. . . Just let me get to the end . . . please . . . I wish I never
started . . . Why do I want to be funny and tell jokes? . . . I hate
telling jokes . . . I hate it . . . I can't tell jokes . . . I'll never be
able to tell them . . . I've never told them so why did I insist?
. . . I loathe it . . . I'm going hot and cold . . . why on earth do
I give myself this torture? . . .

HAL: So vat happened? *I wish I could tell jokes . . . He's so easy
and relaxed in front of his wife . . . maybe I can think of one
. . . now let me see . . .*

DONNA: *I wonder how much time he really spends in bars . . . Does
he find shiksas in there . . . maybe, they're so easy. They drop
their panties at any excuse, loose dirty sluts . . .*

FRANK: Yeah, so the Jew stays for the last show and the usherette
says . . .

DONNA: *A real shiksa usherette with a short skirt and she probably
made a date with him in the bar . . .*

FRANK: So the usherette says to the Jew after seeing him in there for the third showing . . . she says . . . 'Jesus Christ! you here again' . . . hahahaha –

MOTHER-IN-LAW: Yours is with the milk . . .

FRANK: Ma! Later! You see, she thought he was Jesus Christ!

MOTHER-IN-LAW: You have half a sugar . . .

FRANK: Ma! Not now! No, not really, though for the sake of the joke he pretends to believe that she thought he was Jesus Christ . . .

MOTHER-IN-LAW: . . . and yours is black . . .

FRANK: Ma!!! Later!!! . . . Or that he thought that she thought that she thought he was . . . 'cause he was there three times for the three movies . . .

HAL: I think we have the wrong coffee . . . (Exchanges his cup with FRANK's.)

FRANK: . . . so she said . . . hawhawhaw . . . 'J.C., you here again!!' No! Of course she didn't think he was . . . it was an expression . . .

(Pause.)

DONNA, HAL and MOTHER-IN-LAW: Ooooooohhh . . . hahahaha-hahahahahahahaha . . .

HAL: *I don't get it . . . I wasn't paying attention . . . I was thinking of a joke to tell and I missed the tag line . . . And now he thinks I'm not too bright . . . Can he see the blank stare in my eyes? . . . I have to fake it . . . Hawhawhawhawhawhaw! . . .*

FRANK: *I fucked it up . . . My mind went in the middle . . . I was going well and my mind went . . . I didn't make it clear . . . and then she came in with her fucking coffee fucking milk her fucking sugar, fuck you!!! . . . Oh, God . . . my stomach aches . . . my voice is going . . .* (Cough, cough.)

HAL: Haw haw! that's good . . . *My laugh is unconvincing . . . He knows I didn't get it . . . He's looking at me like I'm a killjoy, one that spoils the party. I'm not free any more . . . I was having a good time . . . He's staring at me like he'll never have me round again . . .* Good, Frank!

FRANK: *He's looking at me like I'm crazy . . . He's thinking I'm crazy . . . I'm sweating . . . He's staring at my sweat and wondering about it . . . They're all staring at my sweat. I'll slowly take a handkerchief out and mop it casually . . .*

HAL: *He's staring at me waiting for me to do something . . . tell a joke or what I do with myself . . . I'm stuck . . . I'm stuck in life . . . I can't move or open my mouth . . . my jaw feels clamped . . . Hahahahahahahahaha . . .*
FRANK: *Can't find my handkerchief.*
HAL: *I feel like dying.*
FRANK: *What's Donna doing? . . .*
DONNA: *It's gone very quiet . . . I don't like to interfere when the men are speaking . . . I like to listen. I don't want to be the focus of attention . . . I've got nothing to say but when I do. Sometimes. When I'm being myself I've got plenty to say. But when they are talking I don't sound important . . . I sound stupid . . . But I could say something now! . . . Now is the chance . . .*
(ALL are fixed in a tense stance.)
FRANK: *For God's sake, speak, Donna!!*
HAL: *May the earth open up.*
DONNA: *Now, what can I say . . . umhf? . . . So, Hal, what else do you do at nights? . . .*
HAL: At nights! Nights!? (Cough.) Sorry . . . hmmmm . . . yes, at night . . . (Cough, cough.) Yes, well, at nights . . . Cough, cough.) Yes, well, as you were saying . . . at night . . . (Cough, cough.) Yes, well, at nights . . .
DONNA: Frank . . . help me, please . . .
FRANK: . . . Yeah . . .
HAL: . . . at nights, well . . . (Cough, cough.) Nights are so . . . (Cough, cough.) The thing about nights . . . (Cough, cough.) You see, nights . . .
FRANK: *This is a beautiful evening!!!* (Smells a huge fart.) Oh, God . . . Donna! Did you leave the gas on again? . . .
(Blackout.)

SCENE 2

DONNA: Hold me, Frank . . . don't just sleep . . . kiss me goodnight . . . don't just lie there like a lump . . . I might as well be alone . . .

FRANK: Hmmmf . . . hummmf . . . g'nigh' . . .

DONNA: Frank . . . kiss me goodnight . . . come on turn over . . .

FRANK: Tirrrrreeed . . .

DONNA: Then just kiss me and say goodnight, darling . . .

FRANK: G'nigh', daarrrrling . . .

DONNA: Look at me and say it . . . turn your head . . .

FRANK: *Oh, for fuck's sake . . . I just want to bury myself in sleep . . . just want to drag sleep over me like a sack and die in it until the morning . . . It was a terrible night but at least I did it . . . Now sleep . . . that's what I need, but she keeps asking to be kissed . . . 'Kiss me . . . kiss me . . . kiss me' . . . It's like a goldfish coming at you every time you stand still . . . It's kiss kiss like I was giving resuscitation . . . What is it about the kisses? . . . It's enough already . . . The mouth keeps coming at me followed by the face . . . Sure I love her but tell you the truth I can't shtipp it in any more . . . Sometimes I roll over . . . you know, I've got to make a gesture and stick it in . . . I think of the shiksa in the bar . . . I see her with those tits ripe to plop out like melons . . . so I roll over but it's difficult . . . but I've got a card index to help out . . . the chick in the bus who kept crossing her legs . . . the one who eyed me walking down the street with the kids . . . the girl who smiled at me on the beach all those years ago . . . What might have happened if I made a move always fascinated me . . . so I go through it as I roll over . . . Her legs on the beach . . . long . . . long beautiful legs . . .*

(FRANK kisses DONNA perfunctorily and climbs aboard.)

There . . . there . . . ouch . . . ow! what are you wearing? . . . ouch! . . .

DONNA: Ouch . . . ow! . . . here let me do it . . . there . . . *I want to be raped . . . Sometimes I want the garbagemen to throw me on the bed in the morning after the lump has gone to work and just use* me . . . the three of them . . . and I know they've been eyeing me . . . They empty the garbage cans and I'm still in my nightdress . . . I know they're horny for me . . . They smile and talk after they've gone about the dirty things they'd like to do to me . . . tear my nightie off . . . put their hands all over . . . grab me and tear me to pieces . . . examine and explore me . . . all hungry and sweaty and dirty . . . Sometimes the lump next to me rolls over and sticks his end in and moves it about a bit . . . big favour . . . I let him because he needs to do his duty . . . tell you the truth I'm bored . . . but I want him to do it so I can think of the garbage man . . . taking my panties off and thrusting against me . . . Oh, no . . . he's pulling them down . . . the dirty beast . . . I hope they're clean . . . who cares . . . I'm abandoned . . . I want the two but I resist . . . a bit . . . One of them has already got his cock rubbing against me and the other is kissing me furiously . . . crazily . . . unbelieving his good luck . . . furious and hard . . . passionate as if he might be dreaming all this and want to grab it all before it evaporates . . . Oh, their faces are rough and I'm brittle and soft . . . yielding to all their terrible demands. I give in . . . I'm melting . . . oh!!!! They're doing terrible things to me . . . no . . . not that . . . Oh, it's terrible . . . You're so hungry . . . And they all come at me, each satisfying his scummy lust on me . . . oh, using me . . . ripping me apart with their hot burning lusts . . . oh . . . I'm swimming in it . . . ooh, it's wonderful . . . oh! . . . ooh! . . . ooh! . . .

FRANK: *I excite her like mad . . . so I've got to do it . . . Sometimes even if I find it a struggle . . . I make an effort . . . Listen, she finds me exciting . . . What can you do? . . . I only wish it was reciprocated on my part . . . So I keep my story going to the very end . . . sometimes I vary the story but I always start with picking her up . . . the beach . . . I start talking . . . We slowly link fingers through the sand . . . It's like thunder . . . I have my arm around her waist . . . It feels slender and small . . . She's smiling . . . I tell her a joke . . . She laughs . . . beautiful white teeth . . . and then she puts her arm around my waist and I love that . . . We have a coffee and under the table I can feel her knee brush against mine . . . We're in her room now and she throws herself on to the sofa carelessly . . . Her skirt rides up . . . I join* her . . . *Suddenly I'm kissing her, soft slushy wet mushy kisses and her legs are so strong and fine and she opens them slightly as I kiss her and my hand is crawling up the inside of her thigh which feels like satin and cool and my heart pounds like it's ready to break and now her hand is on my thigh and her fingers gently slipping down into my groin which is packed and now my hands are climbing higher, higher and her legs feel stronger and the thighs powerful and suddenly I feel this enormous . . .* (HAL appears from under the sheets.) *What's happening here? . . . Why are you in my fantasy, Hal? . . . Go away . . . I want the soft squishy sweet succulent . . . not this hard thick big thing . . . go away . . . get out of my fantasy.*

HAL: *But I am your fantasy . . . Relax, don't fight it . . . No one knows . . . only you . . . Even I don't know . . .*

FRANK: *You sure?*

HAL: *Of course. I'm only a fantasy . . . They're supposed to be good for you . . .*

FRANK: *But only in fantasy, you understand . . . This is to go no further . . . I couldn't even think of it in reality . . . Phahhh, it would make me sick . . . yuk! The idea of even kissing another man . . . let alone the other stuff . . .*

HAL: *That's why it's a fantasy . . . You don't even have to smell it . . .*

FRANK: *Don't be so vulgar . . .*

HAL: *Come on . . . Enjoy it without the pain and the guilt . . . Enjoy my big beauty . . .*

FRANK: *God, Hal . . . It's so big . . . and firm . . . mmmmmm . . . go on then, Hal . . . Stick it in and get it over with . . . quickly . . . HaHmmhmmmhmmmhmmhmmhmm!*

(HAL disappears.)
Was that nice for you?

DONNA: Yes, honey . . . Was it OK for you . . . ?

FRANK: Yeeeh . . . g'night . . .

DONNA: 'Night . . .

(Blackout.)

ACT II

SCENE I

FRANK: *I'm afraid . . . I'm afraid of my rates going up . . . I'm afraid to go to the door and look at the bills . . . I'm afraid of brown envelopes . . . I'm afraid of not having enough money . . . Money . . . I want it and need it . . . It gives me peace of mind . . . I work all day for money and I work hard to make more . . . I sell hard and give value . . . I've got a technique when I sell . . . I'm not afraid . . . not so much . . .* It's a beautiful piece of cloth . . . eighteen-ounce gabardine . . . look no crease . . . *I'm afraid to look at the tax demand . . . I'm afraid I'll never make enough . . . What is life but working every day and never quite doing it?* . . . I can get you as much of this as you want . . . last of the range, that's why we're knocking it out cheap . . . Listen, it's a job lot . . . We made a deal . . . What can I say? . . . We bought up a lot . . . so we sell low . . . *How do you start a business?* . . . *I'm afraid to start one because then you could lose everything . . . But what's to be afraid of? . . . You can't die . . . take a risk . . .* So how's Monte? . . .

GEORGE: Fine . . . fine . . . still at college . . .

FRANK: Wonderful! He's a beautiful kid . . . he's clever . . .

GEORGE: Yeah . . . he's taking his degrees in languages . . .

FRANK: No kidding . . .

GEORGE: Yeah . . . he wants to do United Nations work . . . how about that . . .

FRANK: What, like translating and meeting important people? . . .

GEORGE: More like relief work in distressed areas . . .

FRANK: What a kid . . . like he's got some kinda . . .

GEORGE: Moral scruples.

FRANK: Yeah . . . *Wish I had said that . . .*

GEORGE: Not interested in money . . . crazy kid . . . thinks we're all so obsessed by it and we don't look any happier for it . . . so he wants to do some good . . .

FRANK: He knows there's more to life . . . right . . .

23

GEORGE: That's right . . . he could make a fortune . . . brains coming out of his ears . . . take over the business . . . It's a huge turnover now that we're into ladies' underwear . . .
FRANK: You were wise . . . it's a very good line . . . always changing . . .
GEORGE: But he didn't want to end up like us two shmocks, eh!?
FRANK: No . . . that's for sure . . . Hey . . . how do you mean? Us two! . . . Haw haw haw . . .
GEORGE: Come on . . . just kill yourself for dough . . . same old talk . . . same old grind . . . What's for next season? . . . Shlapp it out . . . No time to pick up a book . . . enjoy your life . . . just money money money . . . or worry if you're left with stock . . . When did you last see an opera?
FRANK: An opera? . . . Well, to tell you the truth . . . it's not really my cup of tea . . .
GEORGE: What are you reading at the moment?
FRANK: Reading . . . reading? . . . Yeah, well, I just finished a book . . . yeah I just finished one . . . a week ago . . . No, I tell a lie . . . it must be two maybe three weeks . . . yeah . . . It's essential to keep your eye on the world . . . It's not all about dough . . . you're right . . . or you'll turn into a pumpkin . . . hahahahaha!
GEORGE: Or a shmock! . . .
FRANK: That's right . . . we're a pair of shmocks!!
GEORGE: So what was the book you were reading?
FRANK: The book? Oh, it was a great book . . . a very, very good book . . . deep, mind you . . .
GEORGE: *Look at the pathetic shmock . . . He makes me grow old . . . He reminds me of what I might have become . . . so I shudder inside like I might have some of that contamination inside me . . . Tell you the truth, he makes me sick . . . an ass-kissing slug that creeps around . . . but I see him out of pity and to remind myself what not to become . . . I look at his wheedling pathetic face . . . his greasy skin and the kvetch lines ingrained into his forehead . . . his attempts to smarten up . . . his hopes whenever he comes into the buiding . . . To be a salesman is to be a wheedling ingratiating creep . . . because you need . . . all the time you need our goodwill so you can stay alive . . . I hate*

salesman because they make you responsible for their livelihood
. . . I hate the guilt trip they lay on you . . . Look at this fake
trying to remember a book he never read . . . Who could even
bear to live with him? . . . What his poor wife Donna must think
staring at this shuffling wreck with hairs on his collar . . . his
yellow face . . . Why do I hate him so much? . . .

FRANK: *I wish I was on a beach sitting in the sun with a book and
maybe a Martini on the side . . . I am trying to remember a book
I read recently . . . When was the last time I read a book? . . . I
don't remember . . . I come here to push my stuff and I get put on
the spot . . . Fuck him, the smug bastard . . . Where does he get
off calling me a shmock? . . . He's a shmock . . . But look at
him all comfortable . . . sitting by the Sunday pool while the kids
play Pac-man in the playroom . . . Look at his greasy face well
lined in comfortable dinners and arrogant airs like he owns me
because maybe his money buys something from me which he needs
anyway . . . So I have to kiss his ass 'cause he spends a few
bucks . . . I have to suffer this ignorant fat pig telling me I'm a
shmock because his ability to be greedy is bigger than mine . . .
Who is he to make me sweat? . . . Don't I do enough sweating?
. . . Up yours, you fat greasy bastard . . .*

GEORGE: *Good, soon I'll take lunch . . . When creepo is gone I'll
saunter down to the deli and order a juicy pastrami sandwich
with the meat hanging out and dripping down the side topped
with some cheese and some nice pickle to crunch . . . then some
strong mustard and swallow the whole thing in rye . . . My
mouth is drooling . . . Maybe I should buy to support his family
. . . But then he's always coming back . . . Then be honest . . .
tell him . . . don't shove your job lines and shmutters here . . .
But then he won't have a good lunch . . . He'll not take maybe as
many orders and return home empty-handed . . . So spread a
little cheer . . . Why do I have to suffer this guilt? . . . The
bastard makes me sick and guilty at the same time . . .*

FRANK: *I'll tell him don't give me your what have you read lately bullshit . . . I don't have to listen to it . . . Shove your orders up your
ass and don't lecture me from your high pulpit of inherited wealth,
you fat greedy smarmy bastard . . . When was the last time you
fucked your wife? . . . I bet you buy $500 tricks, you creep.*

GEORGE: *No more guilt . . . just say no more . . . I don't want your shmutters . . . Be polite, it's down-market stuff and get rid of it once and for all . . .*

FRANK: *Right, here goes . . . Now you'll get the biggest earful you ever heard . . . God, I feel good just in anticipation . . . My heart's pumping like mad . . . You know, George . . .*

GEORGE: Yeah, Frank . . . you remember the book now . . . haw haw haw . . .

FRANK: No . . . I've something on my mind I want to say . . .

GEORGE: Oh, yeah . . . good . . . spit it out . . .

FRANK: *You fat greasy stinking lousy smug creep . . . I'd like to kick your ass into next week . . . Don't you ever dare talk to me in your patronizing manner . . . I'm a human being you whoremonger . . . I haven't said this yet . . . I'm just practising.*

GEORGE: *If I invest a quarter-million in silver this month . . . ummmmm . . .*

FRANK: *You vile parasite . . . you're hated . . .*

GEORGE: *I'll go down to the brokers' after my lunch . . .*

FRANK: *Everybody loathes you, you slimy idiot . . .*

GEORGE: *No . . . go before the sandwich and finish your lunch peacefully . . .*

FRANK: *I even hear you letch the salesmen's wives, you dirty whoremonger.*

GEORGE: *Haven't visited Shirley for a while . . .*

FRANK: *I'm gonna tell you now . . .*

GEORGE: *Straight after work . . . I'll book an appointment . . .*

FRANK: *Right . . . now let it out . . .* Y'know, George . . .

GEORGE: So, you were er . . . saying, Frank . . .

FRANK: Listen, George . . .

DONNA: (Enters with MOTHER-IN-LAW) *Don't say it, Frank . . . We've got the health insurance to pay this month . . . for all four of us . . . plus the car needs fixing and the roof leaks . . . Don't throw away our first Christmas holiday to Miami . . . You promised me . . . And mother needs back treatment . . .*

FRANK: *Shit to that.*

DONNA: *Don't think just of yourself . . . don't . . . swallow a little pride . . .*

FRANK: *I'm poisoned on swallowing so much pride . . .*

DONNA: *Ignore him.*
FRANK: *But I'm not a man if I keep up this game* . . .
DONNA: *You were a man last night.*
FRANK: *Yeah . . . I was . . . wasn't I?* . . .
HAL: (Enters.) *That's because of me* . . .
FRANK: *Get out* . . .
HAL: *You liked me then* . . .
DONNA: *What does he mean, Frank?* . . .
FRANK: *Nothing . . . nothing* . . .
MOTHER-IN-LAW: *Tell him, the vstinkiner momsa, and he'll have more respect . . . Don't be a worm all your life . . . In front of your mother-in-law you should be a warrior . . . and what would your mother think, God rest her soul?* . . .
FRANK: *What do you care about my mother? . . . Did you see her when she was dying in the hospital?* . . .
MOTHER-IN-LAW: *Ah! now it comes out! Frank, dollink, I was ill myself with gallstones, God forbid it should happen to you! . . . But still from my sickbed I got up and made borscht for your mother, the Russian kind . . . Didn't I, Donna, didn't I? . . . God rest her soul . . . that borscht kept her going* . . .
FRANK: *Stop it, all of you . . . Shut up . . . Go way . . . I'll do what I want to do . . . I'll tell him for once in my life I'm gonna stand up for myself . . . You know what, George?* . . .
GEORGE: Yeah . . . tell me about it, old boy . . .
DONNA: (Voice offstage) *Frank, don't do it . . . The microwave . . . the second TV in Jennifer's bedroom . . . the VCR . . . the weekend at the Golden Nugget three nights for the price of two . . . the cuisinart . . . the four-wheel drive . . . the computer for Josh* . . .
FRANK: I remember the book now . . .
GEORGE: Oh, yeah . . . *Shirley or Susan?* . . . What?
FRANK: 'How to increase your Earning Power' . . .
GEORGE: Good for you . . . Frank . . .
    (Blackout.)

SCENE 2

FRANK: (In the style of a nightclub comic) *Like it must be paradise to be without a kvetch . . . a place where you kvell . . . Enough of that . . . I had it right up to here . . . like a drum beating the same rhythm in your head . . . boom boom boom . . . Say, I was in a bar, and there was an Englishman, an Irishman and a Jew . . . Oh, you've heard that one . . . oh . . .*
(Chorus of HAL, DONNA, GEORGE and MOTHER-IN-LAW improvise supportive commentary on FRANK's next speech.)
That's a nice stereo . . .

CHORUS: *Ooohh –*

FRANK: *Yeah, that's a beaut . . . amplifier and speakers with a receiver and turntable . . . a tape deck with Dolby too . . .*

CHORUS: (Awe) *Ooohh –*

FRANK: *Yeah, you need that and a switch for metal or chrome . . . What the hell's that?*

CHORUS: *I dunno –*

FRANK: *God, look at those switches . . . You need to go to night school just to learn how to use the fucking thing . . .*

CHORUS: *Hahahaha . . .*

FRANK: *It's a beaut . . . silver and black . . .*

CHORUS: *Tssssss . . .*

FRANK: *It's like a spaceship . . . in the living room it would look great . . . yeah . . .*

CHORUS: *Yeah . . .*

FRANK: *I'd get some opera . . . $600 . . .*
(Whistle from CHORUS.)
It's not cheap . . . but it's state of the art . . . nah . . .

CHORUS: *Nah . . .*

FRANK: *Our stereo's OK . . . but the sound must be like a dream . . . Dolby stereo with room for four speakers . . .*
(Big gasp from CHORUS.)
Then I'd wire two in the kitchen . . .

CHORUS: *Yeah . . . yeah . . .*

FRANK: *But then I'd need to get the builders in . . . shit!*

CHORUS: *Shit!*
FRANK: *Those bastards would charge a fortune . . .*
CHORUS: *Bastards!*
FRANK: *Maybe I'd do it myself . . . Why not? . . .*
CHORUS: *Why not?*
FRANK: *But then I'd have to pull up the floorboards . . .*
CHORUS: *Uh-oh . . .*
FRANK: *And drill a hole . . . I'd have to buy a drill . . . nah . . .*
CHORUS: *Nah . . .*
FRANK: *Who needs it? . . . I do! . . . $600 . . . I can put it on Visa . . .*
CHORUS: *Yeah . . .*
FRANK: *My stereo's OK . . . My stereo's old . . . nah . . .*
CHORUS: *Nah . . .*
FRANK: *Yeah! . . .*
CHORUS: *Yeah . . .*
FRANK: *I'd like a bit of luxury . . . but it's crazy . . . look at it . . .*
CHORUS: *Oooohh . . .*
FRANK: *Man's genius in electronics . . .*
CHORUS: *Wow . . .*
FRANK: *Maybe I'll put it in the kitchen . . . We eat and spend time in there . . .*
CHORUS: *Eh . . .*
FRANK: *And wire the speakers in the living room.*
CHORUS: *Ayyy . . .*
FRANK: *No, make it a showpiece in the living room . . .*
CHORUS: *Showpiece, showpiece!*
FRANK: *I wonder if I could use a drill . . . then I'd have to pull up the carpet . . .*
CHORUS: *Uh-oh . . .*
FRANK: *She'd go crazy . . . it's fitted . . . wall to wall . . . Nah! . . .*
CHORUS: *Nah, nah . . .*
   (FRANK, HAL and MOTHER-IN-LAW exit, mumbling. DONNA and GEORGE are left on stage.)
GEORGE: So, you want to grab a bite to eat? . . .
DONNA: Sure . . . uh-hunh . . . I guess so . . .
GEORGE: How does Italian sound? . . .
DONNA: I love Italian . . .

(FRANK, HAL and MOTHER-IN-LAW cross the stage mumbling as DONNA and GEORGE sit.)

GEORGE: *I'm nervous . . . I didn't sell much last week . . . Business is down and silver slumped . . . I think I've got a lump in my guts . . . Is it a growth? . . . My wife's leaving me for a shvartzer who used to wait tables . . . I'm free again but . . . a salesman's wife . . .*

(HAL enters as a waiter.)

HAL: Buona sera . . . two for dinner? . . . *Thanks for coming in a half-hour before we close . . . assholes . . .* Can I take your order? . . .

GEORGE: We're not quite ready . . .

HAL: Something to drink? . . .

GEORGE: Oh, I dunno . . . Do you want something, honey? . . .

DONNA: Oh, I dunno . . .

HAL: Some wine perhaps . . . red or white? . . .

GEORGE: Which would you like, honey? . . .

DONNA: Oh, I don't care . . . whichever you want . . .

GEORGE: Red . . . do you like red? . . .

DONNA: Red's fine . . .

GEORGE: You want the white, don't you? . . .

HAL: *Make up your minds, you ignorant creeping turds . . .*

DONNA: Whichever you want . . . white is fine . . .

GEORGE: You want the red, don't you? . . . Two glasses of red . . .

DONNA: *I hate red wine . . .*

HAL: Coming right up . . . *I hope it rots your liver . . . I hope you choke on it . . . I hope your kidneys turn to mush . . .* Uno momento . . .

DONNA: Sorry to hear about your wife . . .

GEORGE: I should worry . . . Listen, maybe it's a blessing . . .

DONNA: *He's OK . . . he's quite nice . . . but I don't want to be a stopgap . . . I'm impressing him . . . but don't go to bed on the first time out . . .*

GEORGE: Y'know, Donna . . . I think we just got too used to each other . . . *Cause she liked a big black dick up her, the filthy slut . . . a huge shvartzer . . . and God forbid even . . . no . . . I can't even look at it in my thoughts . . . yeah, go on . . . see it*

. . . *just think about it for a moment . . . no . . . look at it and then it will go away . . . face it . . . draw a picture . . . yaaaaaaaaaa!!!* . . . So we decided to have a trial separation.
DONNA: Yeah, my husband . . . well, we fight a lot . . . *Oh dear, maybe I shouldn't have said that . . . He'll think I'm difficult . . .*
GEORGE: Oh yeah . . . fight, fight . . . yeah . . . ha ha! . . . *That's all I need . . . a trouble maker.*
(Chorus of the Fearful appear against the wall in identity parade.)

HAL: *I'm afraid . . . I fear . . . I'm lonely . . . I want . . . I need . . . I must . . . I hunger . . . I feel . . . I desire . . . friends . . . yeah . . . I need friends . . . I won't tell you this because this is embarrassing but I am going out of my mind with loneliness . . .*
FRANK: *I'm afraid . . . I fear . . . I was on the seventeenth floor today and a window was open . . . and there was nothing but space between me and the deck and I kept seeing myself flying through . . . like in the movies . . .*
DONNA: *I'm afraid . . . What will happen? He doesn't love me . . . He leaves me alone . . . I'm getting old . . . I must be loved . . . I'm neglected and shrivelled from it . . .*
GEORGE: *I'm afraid . . . I can't pay alimony . . . My taxes are awful . . .*
HAL: *I'm desperate . . . I can't breathe . . . I am not popular . . . I have few friends . . . few . . . but I am not liked . . . not popular . . . get nervous . . . not funny . . . not handsome . . . not suave . . . ugly . . . plain . . . ordinary . . . simple . . .*
GEORGE: *And I can't keep it up . . . I couldn't get it up there last night . . . So what? . . . So what? . . . I didn't feel right . . . I couldn't get it stiff!! I couldn't say this to anyone . . . I couldn't speak these thoughts even to my shrink . . . I daren't even think it to myself . . . but I'm afraid of not having a stiff prick . . .*
FRANK: *I saw myself sail through space and hit the deck . . . like a hand was pulling me out or beckoning me . . . a soft invisible hand gathered me up and I was flying . . . What a thrill . . . a five-second thrill . . . That's a good one . . .*
DONNA: *I want to escape . . . I'll find a room but I'm afraid . . . I'll*

be lonely . . . I'll sit there . . . I'm not so attractive any more . . . I've only one tit . . . Who will desire me now? . . . How can I be alone and undesired? . . . I'm bored . . . so bored . . . I hate . . . The day starts and I hate the light threatening me with another empty day . . .

HAL: *But I die in company . . . I have to think out the lines before I say them . . . It doesn't gush out like a spring . . . like a torrent . . . but within I have a waterfall . . . a giant explosion could come gushing out . . . but then an iron door clamps shut on it . . .*

GEORGE: *I can't say this to anyone . . . So I pulled this hooker . . . this shiksa . . . and I started but my will collapsed in my dick . . . My soul and my will is in my dick and it collapsed and so my spirits collapsed if the dick is the barometer of my will . . .*

DONNA: *I'll have an operation . . . I hear they can make one now . . . It's simple . . . Yeah, but costs an arm and a leg just to get a pair of decent tits . . . Yeah, but supposing it fails . . . or looks worse . . . Oh, I don't know . . .*

FRANK: *Stood there with an empty order book and the window beckoning . . . So this is the life . . . to shlapp my guts up and down and lick ass to keep the shreik at home and for what? . . .*

HAL: *So I escape to my room and sit and sit . . . I'm sorry for myself . . . See yourself growing fat in the mirror . . . stare . . . smoke a cigarette . . .*

DONNA: *I'm afraid . . . I fear . . . I want . . . I need . . . I ache . . . I hunger . . . I cry . . . I sicken . . .*

FRANK: *So the window was a ticket . . . like a cheque that I can cash . . . splattered out on the sidewalk and the crowd . . . circling and feasting on the mess . . . as my skull lay cracked open like an egg . . . So I looked out at all the space I would soon occupy but I was afraid . . .*

GEORGE: *And so I'm afraid . . . each new woman inspires the greatest terror . . . that I'll shrink because I lack . . . or feel I lack . . . some kind of power . . . Maybe I'm a fruit . . . no . . . God forbid . . .*

(Blackout and return to restaurant.)

You're sure he doesn't know? . . .
DONNA: No! . . . he doesn't even suspect . . .

GEORGE: Donna, I love you!
DONNA: No, no, don't say that . . .
GEORGE: I have to tell you . . . I have to . . .
DONNA: No, don't George . . . I can't do this . . .
GEORGE: You love me too . . . you know you do . . . don't you? . . .
DONNA: But he comes to you for orders . . .
GEORGE: So . . . I buy his shmutters even when I don't want them . . . to help you, Donna . . . Donna, come on let's go to bed . . . *Hopefully she'll say no but then at least she'll know how much I care . . . To tell you the truth I don't feel like it . . . I'm off it . . . but a cuddle I'd like and maybe cook me a meal . . . Sick of having to deliver on demand . . .*
DONNA: I can't, George . . .
GEORGE: *That's a relief* . . . Awww! Come on . . .
DONNA: Don't ask me again . . .
GEORGE: You know I'll never stop . . . *Phew, what a relief* . . .
DONNA: And after . . . huh . . . after you've got what you want . . .
GEORGE: That's what you think of me . . . I respect you, Donna . . . as a woman . . . What . . . you think at my age I'm looking for one-night stands? . . . You know I love you . . . from the minute I saw you at the annual Christmas party with your husband . . . I fell . . . what can I say? . . . You're a desirable woman, Donna, but I respect your wishes . . . *So I don't have to fuck and I come across as a horny guy . . . brilliant!!*
DONNA: *I'm afraid that when he sleeps with me . . . I've got only one tit . . . That's a lot to handle . . . Especially if you are not in love . . . He'll be put off . . . What if he really loves me? . . . so what's a little breast? . . . a piece of tissue with a piece of cork on the end . . . So men act like nirvana lies in a perfect-shaped pendulous breast . . . fat . . . juicy . . . like a great hanging fruit . . . like a melon . . . ready to burst and wobbling under a thin shirt with nipples like armour-plated bullets . . . a whole fat breast hanging in his hand like he was weighing an avocado . . . I mustn't get myself into this state . . . It's silly . . . But he holds each breast and examines me . . . his eyes narrowing and closing*

in like a little satellite landing on the moon . . . scanning the terrain for the best landing site . . . His mouth's closing in now . . . and the exhaust blast brings up little goose pimples on the terrain . . . Now he accelerates forward . . . The moon very slowly turns on a gentle pivot . . . as if by gravitational pull and his jaw . . . rough . . . two days' growth . . . opens wide, a dark inferno where a massive snake lolls wet and expectant . . . His lips, like crimson curtains pull back . . . And the moon . . . all white and glowing in its fullest state as the mouth opens and the snake darts out . . . and . . . with the tip of that snake-like tongue lifts the cork and gently places it in his warm mouth . . . where it gets hot and hard inside his teeth and he chews and bites gently . . . now harder . . . now harder still and then slowly . . . inch by inch . . . gently . . . gradually . . . sucks it all back swollen into his mouth again and he looks like he is blowing up a big balloon and then he lets it whoosh out once more . . . And then the whole process is repeated . . . Yeah, it would be nice . . .

(She has climbed on to the table during her speech, which is now in her kitchen.)

FRANK: I'm home, honey . . . What are you doing on the table? . . .

DONNA: Ohh! I thought you were coming home late . . . It's not ready . . .

FRANK: Listen, who cares? . . . Give me a beer, honey . . . *That dream I had the other night . . . about Hal, you know . . . That's bad . . . I mean that must be there in my subconscious . . . I never knew I had any of that in me . . . It's disgusting what filth I have up there in my brain* . . .

DONNA: There's no beer in the fridge . . . We don't often keep beer . . . You never want it normally . . .

FRANK: What do you mean normally? Many times I have brought home a six-pack . . .

DONNA: Yeah, but you used it weeks ago . . .

FRANK: So you can't say we don't keep it . . .

DONNA: Not normally . . . since when are you a beer-drinking man? . . .

34

FRANK: Since when! Since when! Do I have to be an alcoholic to drink beer?
DONNA: We got wine . . . wine we got . . .
FRANK: What wine we got?
DONNA: The wine we use for pasach . . .
FRANK: I'll go out and get a beer.
DONNA: Frank?
FRANK: Huhn?
DONNA: Oh, Frank . . .
FRANK: Wad!!
DONNA: Why are you drinking?
FRANK: I dunno . . . 'Cause I'm afraid of being a fairy . . . 'cause I have dreams of Hal . . . I just felt like one . . .
DONNA: It's not like you . . . Is something wrong?
FRANK: Nah, I'm just fed up . . .
DONNA: With me??
FRANK: Hell, no!
DONNA: With what, then? . . .
FRANK: With the work . . . Tell you the truth I'm sick of hustling to that slimy dress manufacturer . . .
DONNA: Which one? . . .
FRANK: The one we met at that awful Christmas party, who said come up and show me your samples . . . the slimy bastard . . . I'm sick of seeing his face . . . I'm sick to hell of it and sometimes I just want to smash him . . . just want to take my two fists and go pow pow pow pow pow, take that, you smelly greasy farty bag of scum . . . I don't need your money . . . That's what I need, Donna . . . Oh, Donna . . .
DONNA: He sticks it in me, Frank.
FRANK: Break a chair over his head . . . I hold myself back . . .
DONNA: He pulls my panties off and shoves his cock in . . .
FRANK: How dare he look down on me as some kind of Peon . . . He makes money out of me! . . .
DONNA: He doesn't even mind my one tit . . . says it's cute . . .
FRANK: He makes big profits out of me . . . Mr Greasy . . .
DONNA: Says he can concentrate better on one tit . . .
FRANK: I'm a man, Donna . . . I'll not be spat upon . . .
DONNA: I'm a woman and need a good screw from time to time.

FRANK: It's not enough to shlapp my guts out from one end of town to another begging to be seen like a leper . . . but I make money for them . . . finding them cheap discounted lines . . .
DONNA: Shut up! Shut up! Shut up! Shut up! Shut up! . . . Shut up!
FRANK: Donna??
DONNA: He sticks it into me . . . the manufacturer . . . I had to tell you . . .
FRANK: Wad!!!? Wayasay!!? Wadya saying . . . Wad's coming out of your mouth??? Donna, am I hearing you??? Is that you??
DONNA: Yeah . . . listen . . . it's kvetching me and I have to let it out . . . that fat greasy manufacturer . . . the one who bosses you around . . . well, he really likes me and though he's screwing you, metaphorically of course, he's screwing me . . . so we're both being screwed so put that in your mouth and smoke it . . .
FRANK: Donna . . . I never heard you talk like that.
DONNA: I decided to kick kvetching . . . and suddenly like a dam . . . it all comes tumbling out.
FRANK: You kicked *kvetching*!!!!! How?????
DONNA: By deciding to do what I want and let the guilt go fuck itself . . . you know . . . at that Christmas party for the wholesalers . . . you introduced me and he's been after me ever since but I've been afraid 'cause of my one tit and he's been afraid in case he couldn't make it after his wife walked out . . . So we put our two minuses together and came up with a plus . . . It's OK . . . I told you . . . I let it out . . . I won't kvetch any more . . . I'm sorry, Frank . . . I'm sorry . . . My suitcases are packed . . . and your dirty laundry has been done . . . and there's three pints of milk in the fridge . . .
(DONNA leaves.)
FRANK: *Deciding what I want and let the guilt go fuck itself . . . hmmmnn . . .*
(HAL enters and rings the doorbell.)
Oh, hi, Hal . . . Thanks for coming over . . . Sorry for calling so early . . .

HAL: It's all right . . .
FRANK: Cup of coffee? . . .
HAL: Only if it's made . . .
FRANK: Well, I can make it . . .
HAL: No, no . . .
FRANK: You want instant? . . .
HAL: No, I'm OK . . .
FRANK: You want some raisin toast? . . .
HAL: No . . . thanks . . .
FRANK: A muffin? . . .
HAL: No . . . really . . . I just had breakfast . . .
(Awkward pause.)
FRANK: So you see, Hal . . . she's been betraying me all this time . . .
HAL: You can't trust them, Frank . . .
FRANK: I didn't know what to do or who to call . . .
HAL: I don't mind . . . I really don't . . . and you should call . . .
FRANK: *What is this? . . . I got a hard-on up to my chin . . . I wish I could tell him how I felt* . . . That's kind of you, Hal . . .
HAL: Hell, kind . . . I've been alone . . . I know what it's like . . . *God, he's manly but I'm afraid in case I'm making a huge mistake . . . Why doesn't he get closer or at least make some signal? . . . Brush my knee or something? . . . Maybe I'll make a move . . .*
FRANK: You do know what it's like . . . *Suppose I revolt him . . . Suppose I'm crazy and he runs out screaming . . . No, I must suffer it . . . These are evil disgusting thoughts but I can't stop thinking about . . . it . . .*
HAL: What will you do?
FRANK: What will I do? . . . I dunno . . . I'm alone . . . at forty I'm alone . . . Like I gotta do it all over again . . . like try to meet girls again . . . at my age . . . like where do you go . . . You know what I'm saying, Hal . . . like I can't go to discos and unless I meet them at maybe a party . . . Where then? . . . And who invites me to parties anyway . . . huh? I mean like I'm lonely, Hal . . . Hal? How do you manage? . . . I mean at my age . . .
HAL: Frank . . . Frank . . .

(HAL puts his hand on FRANK's shoulder.)

DONNA: I'm free now I've left him . . .
GEORGE: Great . . . You told him it was me? . . . Oi!
DONNA: Yeah, let it all out what the hell . . .

(FRANK and HAL in bed.)
FRANK: Hal . . . why don't we set up together? . . .
HAL: Are you sure? . . .
FRANK: May as well . . . only don't spread the word . . . OK? . . . About us . . . I don't need any more kvetches! Hey, Hal . . . you know what? . . . I don't feel as if I have one any more . . .
HAL: Did I help you get rid of it?
FRANK: You sure did . . .
HAL: Kvetches gone now, huh? . . .
FRANK: Oh, yeah . . .
HAL: Y'know, Frank . . . I'll give up my apartment if it's all right with you . . . It's an expensive dump . . . We can split expenses . . . Listen, it'll be so much cheaper . . .
FRANK: Listen, we'll save a fortune . . . *We get on fine . . . but suppose after a while we don't get on so good? . . . I mean it's possible . . . maybe I should move into his and rent mine out . . . but I like my house . . . Shit, I've just got my freedom!*
HAL: You will want to give it a whirl?
FRANK: Er . . . sure, Hal . . .
HAL: Are you sure? . . . I mean, level with me? . . .
FRANK: Yeah, of course I am . . . Let's give it a whirl . . . Hell, it's not the end of the world . . . *Oh, shiiiit!* . . . G'night, Hal . . . *I don't want him to give up his place and I don't want to move . . . What's going on? . . . I should tell him . . . but I don't want him to take it bad . . . but I suggested it . . .*
HAL: Frank . . . aren't you going to kiss me goodnight??
(Slow fade to black – threatening music.)

ACAPULCO

CHARACTERS

KAREN, an average white American from New Jersey
STEVE, an English actor, taciturn, moody
VOYO, Yugoslavian-Russian type, volatile, exuberant, powerful build
BARMAN, faceless, indifferent, a barman anywhere
WILL, New York actor, wiry, dark, satanic, intense with humour
JOHN, Scot living in Mexico, small, wiry, playful, intense but inclining to the philosophic

The play is set in a bar at the Acapulco Plaza Hotel. It's a modern and elaborate place where people sit at the bar or at tables nearby. It's a long bar and should stretch from one end of the stage to the other. The barman should be almost invisible in his movements but always there to serve and never standing idly. The actors form a frieze across the bar, reaching over each other to make their points, ordering drinks to punctuate the long speeches, lighting cigarettes, etc. The acting style should be easy and casual broken up by laughter and the normal behaviour patterns of people relaxing after work.

KAREN: Hey, I saw you at breakfast this morning.
STEVE: Sure, I remember you . . . How are you? You got a nice smile . . .
KAREN: So have you . . . I thought, 'Hey! That guy's smiling at me.' I'm Karen . . . Hi, Steve . . . You seem pretty fit for an older guy . . . Do you work out?
STEVE: No, sometimes, you know, not weights . . . a few situps to keep trim. Used to play a lot of squash . . .
KAREN: So you were smiling at me . . .
STEVE: Well, you've got a lovely smile.
KAREN: You're a handsome guy . . .
STEVE: (Won) Hey . . . you're sweet . . .
KAREN: (To BARMAN) Any matches?
STEVE: Where are you from, Karen?
KAREN: (Lighting a cigarette) What?
STEVE: Where you from?
KAREN: New Jersey . . . It takes me forty-five minutes to get to Manhattan.
STEVE: Do you go there a lot? . . . Do you get into town?
KAREN: It's so dirty.
STEVE: Yeah . . .
KAREN: It's dirty . . . I don't like to go there too much.
STEVE: See any shows?
KAREN: Yeah . . . I saw *Dream Girls*. They were all black.
STEVE: Was it good? . . . I didn't see it.
KAREN: Oh, it was great . . . Look! I bought this ring for my mother . . .
STEVE: Nice . . . Hey! That's nice.
KAREN: Cost me a hundred dollars . . . Cute, huh?
STEVE: It is . . .
KAREN: You have a nice smile . . . I thought, 'Hey! That guy's handsome . . .'
STEVE: Come on . . . I think you have a lovely smile.
KAREN: You got a lady here?
STEVE: Nah!
KAREN: You haven't a lady? A handsome guy like you

STEVE: Haven't found anyone . . . not here . . . no, not really.
KAREN: Hey, where's my friends gone . . . They've shot off . . . Maybe they're by the pool . . . Wanna come? . . . Maybe they're by the pool, drinking. I'll ring the bar . . .
STEVE: You go and see. I'll wait . . .
KAREN: You make sure you do . . .
STEVE: I will.
KAREN: You wanna come . . . drink at the pool?
STEVE: I think the bar is closed . . .
KAREN: I'm a bit woozy . . . Shit . . . Hey, you're nice! How old are you?
STEVE: Whad??
KAREN: Nothing . . .
STEVE: Go on . . . Let it out . . . How old am I?
KAREN: What's your last name?
STEVE: Bennet.
KAREN: Mine's Ryton.
STEVE: What do you do?
KAREN: I'm a telephonist . . . It's my birthday next Friday . . . I'll be twenty-two. Still a baby! How old are you?
STEVE: Forty-five!
KAREN: No! You gotta be kiddin' . . . You could be my dad!
STEVE: Sure, I could . . . Do you like that?
KAREN: I'll go look for friends . . .
   (She goes.)
VOYO: (Who has been listening at the bar nearby) How can you talk to that idiot?
STEVE: She's an idiot . . .
VOYO: How can you talk to that . . .
STEVE: I don't know . . . just a piece between her legs is her passport to immunity . . .
VOYO: She's an idiot . . . Just because she's a woman . . .
STEVE: I wouldn't speak to a man who was such an idiot but I waste my time listening to garbage . . .
VOYO: She's stupid . . . just a typical American bitch who's on vacation and drunk . . . She makes me sick!
STEVE: Yeah, I know . . . We prostitute ourselves for the sake of a quick bang.

VOYO: It's terrible . . . it's terrible what you do . . .
STEVE: What do you want to do?
VOYO: I'll go for a walk. Maybe I'll pick something up.
STEVE: I'll join you later. Where are you going?
VOYO: Maybe I'll look in the disco.
STEVE: OK. I'll join you later . . .
VOYO: See ya . . .
(He leaves.)
KAREN: Where'd your friend go?
STEVE: He went to meet someone . . .
KAREN: He didn't say much . . .
STEVE: He's Russian . . . He doesn't understand English . . .
KAREN: He's Russian! Hey! What's he do?
STEVE: He works with me. We're together in this picture.
KAREN: Do you know Stallone? . . .
STEVE: Yeah . . . I have to work with him.
KAREN: He's got a real beautiful wife . . .
STEVE: Did you read that in a magazine?
KAREN: No . . . Somebody told me . . . or I read it. So you play a Russian?
STEVE: Yeah . . .
KAREN: Do a Russian accent for me . . .
STEVE: (In Russian accent) I am so pleased to meet you . . .
KAREN: That's good . . . That's very convincing . . . Can I sip your margarita? Just a sip . . . I ran in the sea today . . . I got my shorts wet . . . I went shopping and bought this ring . . . and these shorts . . . I'm ready for a jungle trek . . . Ha! Ha! Ooh! I've got sand all over my legs and feet.
STEVE: You should take a bath.
KAREN: Is that an invitation?
STEVE: (Unenthusiastic) Yeah . . .
KAREN: Oh! I've got sand everywhere . . .
(Blackout. voices:)
STEVE: I'm sorry.
KAREN: It was nice.
STEVE: You sure?
KAREN: Yeah. Really . . . It was great . . . You felt jus
STEVE: OK.

KAREN: Come on . . . I've had a good time . . . Where are my cigarettes? Shit! I left my handbag in the bar . . .
STEVE: It'll still be there . . .
KAREN: Shit! Left everything in it. My driver's licence, Social Security, my boyfriend's photo . . . Shit!
STEVE: I didn't see you with it at the bar.
KAREN: Shit! I had everything in it . . .
STEVE: If it was there they'd find it . . .
KAREN: God! What was I thinking of . . .
STEVE: You took my arm as we left . . . You didn't have a bag.
KAREN: 'Cause I left it at the bar . . .
STEVE: I didn't see one at the bar, I mean . . . We'll find it if it's there . . . The Mexicans are honest. They'll give it in . . .
KAREN: Shit . . . You got to be kidding . . .
STEVE: (Still worried) Was it OK?
KAREN: (Dull) Yeah, it was great . . .
(End of blackout. Back at the bar.)
KAREN: It was about half-hour . . . forty minutes ago.
BARMAN: Sorry, Senorita. There's nothing here.
KAREN: Not now, but maybe somebody handed it over.
BARMAN: No, sorry.
KAREN: Then take my room number . . . Take my room number or I'll have your ass. Pronto! Rapido!
BARMAN: There's no bag here . . . I'm sorry!
KAREN: These guys are crazy, I swear . . . Where's the manager? I left my fucking bag here half an hour . . . maybe forty minutes ago . . . Now, please take my number and call the police . . . Maybe somebody took it there. Everything was in there!
STEVE: How much money did you have?
KAREN: There was no money in it . . . It was personal shit you can't replace. Oh, shit! What a night . . .
STEVE: Sorry about that . . .
KAREN: Yeah, if you hadn't smiled at me, I wouldn't have lost my bag. I had photos and my bloody driving licence . . . My sister will kill me . . .
BARMAN: If somebody hands it in . . . I will call . . .
KAREN: Yeah, OK. Thanks . . . You'd better.

STEVE: I feel responsible . . .
KAREN: Yeah . . . (Blackout.) If you hadn't smiled at me I would still have my bag!

WILL comes into the bar.
WILL: I just came in the bar . . . I was walking past . . . I thought. 'Shall I go in or not?' . . . And you're here! I didn't work today. I didn't know what to do . . . I didn't feel like going to the beach at La Questa. I just didn't feel like it . . . I felt out of it . . . Like I didn't deserve it . . . I would have loved it . . . I mean, I love it down there, but I just hung around this awful beach. Just walked up and down and then I went downtown for a coffee. I felt desperate. Like out of it. You went to La Questa! Was it beautiful there? Did you see the sunset? You just sit and can meditate for hours. Stare at those great breakers rolling in. No tourists. No Americans down there. Just peace. You went down there, eh? I nearly went. I got up . . . Looked at the day, but felt I didn't deserve it. I felt out of it, so I walked around and had a coffee . . . And was walking back when I thought, 'Why not try the bar?' . . . And you're here! Great! That chick you were speaking to. She's a cock-teaser. I saw her in the pool yesterday, and she smiled and came on strong like she was into me. You know, she lightly touched my thigh as she spoke . . . in the pool . . . I just dived in and as I surfaced there she was . . . You know, I haven't been with a woman in three weeks. Like . . . this is Acapulco. You know what I'm saying. Not even been out with one . . . I had a hard-on and I wanted to put it somewhere. And then I saw her talking to the other guys like I was just a piece of furniture . . . I came out of my hotel this morning . . . you know . . . to get a coffee . . . and that stunt guy was walking in the coffee shop with four chicks! Four! I couldn't believe it . . . four of them. You know your mind plays tricks. Fantasies of having the four . . . one at a time . . . So I followed him to the coffee shop and listened at a discreet distance . . . And what a piece of shit I heard . . . And I immediately went off them. Somehow, you know, when you hear the stark reality

of their minds. I felt repulsed. I couldn't go near them, so I felt down. I was walking past and I thought, Why not come in here?' . . . And, like magic . . . You know, you're the only person that I can relate to . . . in the whole fuckin' film . . . The others! The guy playing the sergeant . . . Fuck him . . . and the fuckin' stand-in! I walked past her trailer one morning and she looked nice. You know . . . kind of pretty, so I said, 'Hey! You're looking real pretty today' and do you know what she said? 'Oh, gimme a break.' I was just being friendly . . . She thinks because I'm playing a POW that I'm scum . . . 'Cause I was cast in Mexico and not in Hollywood. And 'cause I'm paid in pesos I'm scum . . . 'Cause we look like scum . . . Locked up in the wooden cage like some kind of animals . . . You know, this is such a goyish picture . . . There's not a Jew in the whole company except me . . . and, of course, you. But we're not like Jews . . . not like those Jews who worry all the time and are accountants . . . We're tough . . . I'm a tough Brooklyn Jew and they know it . . . You know . . . They can't mess around with me. You are tough, too! You came off the streets, right? Stallone's tough, but underneath you know Stallone's a very vulnerable guy. He's an Italian. The Jews and the Italians get on. What did you do today?

STEVE: I've not been to the John in the whole of Mexico . . . I wait and hold it until I get back to the hotel . . . It stinks here . . . Everything stinks . . . So I went out to La Questa and saw the sunset . . . The clouds moved slowly . . . bloody . . . at the edges . . . like cotton-wool seeping slowly . . . like a knife had stabbed a big belly of a cloud . . . and it was slowly going pink and then red . . . I went walking back in the dark . . . There were huge craters in the road from the hurricane, so I walked a bit. And the sky was like shrieking and the clouds were bolting home looking ragged and torn . . . and there was a lagoon on one side and sea on the other . . . and the sea was all rough but the lagoon was like a sheet of glass. I walked and there was junk everywhere . . . Mounds of old rotting coconuts and fruit that had been left to the pigs . . . And the lizards were flicking in and out as I passed near them . . . I heard them scrambling away as they felt my footsteps . . . And I came to the end and there was a forest . . . You know, like a jungle on one side with tall palms and some dirty old huts and a few tables where you could eat and the kids were swimming around in the sunset . . .

WILL: Oh, the sunsets are beautiful!

STEVE: You know . . . on the road there, there is a man with one leg selling water mixed with some fruit juice . . . just standing there all day and I didn't see him sell anything . . . all those large bottles.

WILL: There's every juice in the world there . . . anything . . . and you can drink the water.

STEVE: At the end there's a café called Steve's Place . . . and you can sit there and drink and watch the sunset. Flies buzzing around the kitchen. All open . . . Dogs and cats sniffing around . . . Somebody's always eating something indescribable. But the fish was great! Under the palm umbrella I had the red snapper. It was laid out on the plate like an offering . . . surrounded by sliced tomatoes and onions and under a napkin were hot tortillas made out of flour . . . No, they were made from corn. And it was on a tray. And, as I looked at the sea tearing itself into little pieces against the sand, I prised a piece of fish off with my fork, which pulled away easily, beautifully cooked, and wrapped it in the hot tortilla, perched a tomato on it, onions, and folded it, and then added some salsa. That hot sauce that goes straight for the exit and misses out the middle man. It burns a road right through you. So I sat and shooed the flies and excavated the fish until I left the bones and the head and was careful not to get too close to that thing . . . But two little kids came and asked for the head like it was a luxury for them. They broke it off the spine of the fish and chewed into it, eyes and all. Boy! They were so happy, they were laughing and chewing the head, since it tasted good to them. They were looking at me and laughing as if I had been stupid and thrown away a great treat. It looked really disgusting with its eyes open. Then a dog chewed the bones that they left and then . . . I saw columns of ants descend on the crumbs . . . The sun was, by this time, slowly sinking into the sea . . . like the weight of it was too much. It sank like a swollen bloated belly . . . bulging even more as it sank. Then scorched the sea up and plunged down deep . . . So I paid and left and walked a while. Meanwhile, the little cafés were lit up with their kitchens all open and frying and cooking and chopping tops off coconuts and this guy had this really sharp machete and sliced the top off the coconut like he was taking off a skull and I drank it. It tasted sweet and strange. Then I got a cab and came back. The sunset was gorgeous. Yeah . . . like a multi-coloured tropical flower . . . or like you took a huge sword and stabbed the sea and it spewed blood everywhere with drips hanging off the clouds.

WILL: Sounds like you had a good day . . .

(Blackout.)

JOHN: Of course, I'm in a cage. That's right, but I'm working . . . I'm earning . . . So what I've no lines? But at least I'm near to something going on . . . Listen, my friend . . . we POWs are very important people and we must sit in that cage all day and concentrate . . .

WILL: You can say what you like . . . We're still the scum . . . the background 500 bucks a week and a *per diem*. So think what you like . . . It makes you feel better, but I know the truth . . . we're the Peons cast in Mexico 'cause it's cheaper to pay us in pesos than fly actors from Hollywood. That's the truth!

JOHN: That's in your mind . . . You're the outcast because it's in your head to be an outcast . . . 'I've no lines. I'm a POW and a piece of shit' . . . Well, that's in your head . . . I'm important in this movie . . . The director saw a lot of people for these parts in Mexico City and said, 'You're it!' You are working on *Rambo*. Hey! They're not going to use bums as POWs that Stallone's risking his life to save . . . I'm working and proud to be in it.

WILL: You know the scene when the tarantula walked over my leg . . . just took a slow walk and the director says, 'What's in your mind now?' What's in my fucking mind? . . . I'm nearly dead, locked up for ten years in a cage . . . What's in my fucking mind? 'Nothing,' I felt nothing, I told him . . . He said, 'Keep your eyes open and hold your hands like this.' (Grips fingers inside each other.) What the hell does that mean? (As if pulling fingers) Like this . . . and keep my eyes open and then they put the spider there . . .

JOHN: He can't direct . . . Anyone can see that . . .

WILL: So we do the shot and the spider walks over me. He just walks and walks and when he came to my flesh . . . he stopped. Like he knew there was something different. He walked down the cloth and felt safe, but when it came to my flesh it felt warm . . . He didn't know how to handle it . . . He kinda lifted his leg up . . . like he was stepping on hot coals . . .

JOHN: There are too many directors on this film . . .

WILL: So he said, 'Cut' and came screaming over . . . 'What was in your mind?' he said. I said, 'Nothing', I mean I was dead. 'You ruined the bloody shot . . . you moved your thumb!' I moved my thumb . . . What does this mean, I moved my thumb? . . . I'm doing what I was told . . . I'm lying there . . . I'm holding my fingers like he said and I moved my thumb . . . He's screaming at me . . . 'What are you doing? . . . This is Panavision!' I ruined his shot . . .

JOHN: That's 'cause you're an outcast. He senses you don't care.

WILL: But I care . . . I do . . . I care desperately . . . I'm an actor . . . I've got one line . . . 'He's dead.' So what? That's OK. I'm working . . . I'm not an outcast . . . Nah, it's the people . . . the people here that make you feel like that . . .

JOHN: That's shit! You do that . . . You've got to think of yourself as a god . . . That's what you have to do. You're as good as anyone. You don't think enough of yourself . . . I told Stallone . . . I went up to him . . . I said, 'You look like a man with a problem.' He said, 'You're right!' I said, 'Look at yourself! What you're making here is a Tarzan movie' . . . that's all. I told him . . . He lacks culture.

WILL: You said that?

JOHN: You were there . . . Weren't you there when I said that?

WILL: I was sitting near, but I didn't hear what you were saying . . . I wasn't straining my ears.

JOHN: I said to him . . . 'You're searching for something else and you surround yourself with all these bums . . . these heavies . . . all this muscle . . . but inside all this muscle is a *man* trying to get out . . .'

WILL: You said that to him?

JOHN: No, I didn't say exactly that . . . I said, 'You're looking for something. You lack culture.' I did say that. He said, 'You're right, John.' He said, 'You're my man in Mexico . . .' and that heavy punk that's always around him, wiping his ass for him said, 'Leave him alone.' I said, 'Listen, I can speak to whom I like. This is a free society.'

WILL: Maybe he asked his man to tell you to take off because he didn't like to tell you himself. Maybe he was sick of punks like coming up and giving him advice . . .

JOHN: Bollocks! He loved it . . . He's starving for a bit of human contact . . . The whole place is filled with ass-lickers. He was glad for someone to come up to him and talk to him straight. I told him . . . I said, 'You need to get back on the track.' But he's so surrounded by these toadies he can't see . . . like that guy who's making the documentary. He doesn't know his tit from his asshole. I said, 'What are you shooting?' And he said, 'I don't know yet.' Don't know! I know more about Mexico than he'll ever know . . . I live here and he's making a documentary about filming in Mexico. And he hasn't got a clue!

STEVE: But he's making the doc . . . and you're in a cage!

JOHN: What do you mean . . . ?

STEVE: I mean he's got a budget of maybe half a million to make a thirty-minute doc . . . direct it . . . travel to Mexico on first-class flight . . . have meetings with the producers . . . have the ear of Stallone . . . And where are you? You're sitting in a cage. You're sitting in your cage as background for the film . . . So, who listens or who cares about what you think?

JOHN: Yes, but that's only for now, my friend . . . This film is a matter of convenience and it suits my purpose . . . I have an office in Mexico and I make Mexican documentaries . . .

STEVE: So . . . what are you doing in a cage?
JOHN: It's convenient . . . Things are quiet at the moment. But let me assure you, my friend . . . at six p.m. I am out of the cage and I am making some very useful contacts. I won't always be working in a cage.
STEVE: (Joshing) You will! You'll always be in a cage like he'll always be an outcast . . .
JOHN: But, as I said, this is expedient, my friend, and I have already suggested an idea for Stallone . . .
WILL: Why don't you let him speak! You might learn something!
JOHN: I know we're in cages now. We're all in cages. You're in a cage of your own making . . . Stallone's in a cage . . . Look at him buried in muscle and a victim of the very thing he succeeded in.
WILL: Let the man speak. He was telling us something . . . Go on, you were saying something . . . Maybe we can learn something!
STEVE: What I mean is . . .
(Blackout.)

STEVE: . . . You live all the time for the present.
JOHN: Yes, live for the present for the morrow will take care of itself . . . Live in the now . . . Enjoy your life.
STEVE: Yes, but somehow in the present we make preparations for the future . . . We make houses for the future . . . We put a brick down and then another . . . one on top . . . But you want what you can make now . . . like a nice juicy dinner and get smashed or stoned because you can do it and finish it in one night . . . You only want what you can make now and so tomorrow you will face the same possibilities . . . You want excitement and buzz, to get pissed and shout and maybe go to the disco all night and then a fuck . . . That's all you talk about . . . Well, all right. Not all you talk about but it takes up a lot of your time . . . Eventually your dick becomes your salvation . . . A nice pussy and something to shove in it and the act is complete . . . It's a beginning and it has an end. Find someone . . . get chatting and fuck . . . then sleep . . . get up . . . rub your eyes . . . eat . . . jump in

the studio car . . . 'Hey, what a great night I had!' . . . and get back into the cage all content. It's natural.
JOHN: Oh, come on! . . .
STEVE: It's natural 'cause it's the one thing you can do which has the total world in it and there's no need to plan or think for the future. Like all those things are activities that can be accomplished in one night and you have symbolically created something . . . or made something like an animal that lives for the now . . . That's good, you say, but you carry no concept for the future. (To BARMAN) Another margarita, please.
(They all order drinks of their choice.)
I mean it's good . . . and you feel open and released and you like getting pissed and talking . . . having a good time . . . following your prick for a few moments of transcendental bliss . . . You rub the magic lamp and the genie appears.
WILL: My genie hasn't appeared much lately! . . .
STEVE: And it takes away the emptiness and then you're back in the cage.
JOHN: Listen, my friend, my life's full . . . It's not empty . . . It's packed full every day.
WILL: Let him finish.
STEVE: It's a good life and it feels rich, but there's no pain . . . It's pain that makes you think. You know a bit of pain makes you aware of other things than the shit you spew out . . . Structure. You've got to structure things for the future and by thinking you realize that life is ongoing. It doesn't stop tonight . . . Pain makes you think of life. What it means. Your appetite makes you feel . . . and that needs immediate satisfying. Pain makes you think of how to stop the pain . . . That's why you're in the cage . . . You want to satisfy feelings all the time like an animal. You're caged . . . Happy to be there until you are released and can run around like a mad beast satisfying your appetites . . . The man making the documentary woke up one morning feeling pain . . . He had to express his life on this planet . . . What could he do to express his voice? It gave him pain . . . made him reclusive, anti-social, pensive . . . introverted . . . It was a pain . . . he

had to solve so he planned, thought, observed, analysed . . . became aware and made telephone calls to important men in the industry. These men who have little time for fools cocked an ear and invited him to sit in offices where secretaries are seldom idle. They ate lunch and discussed formulas, plans and budgets. They reached agreements and called each other by their Christian names! And, lo and behold! Funds were set flowing into this project . . . And one day he flew on western airlines, first class, to Acapulco with a TV crew and started filming in the jungle of Mexico a documentary about Stallone . . . And in the background in a dirty cage which stays mainly out of focus are five POWs . . . OOWA . . . out-of-work actors . . . and in a coffee break one of these grimy, one-notch-over-a-crowd workers, comes up and says to this man making the TV . . . 'What line are you taking in this?' And the man, not wishing to get involved in the mêlée or rabble that makes up a movie set, says, 'I'm not sure yet' . . . Then the monkey in the cage released for its night of monkey chat and leaping about squeals . . . with delight . . . and supreme knowledge . . . 'He doesn't know!!' When, in fact, the man didn't wish to talk to a monkey about things . . .

WILL: You see . . . I told you you'd learn something!! You're a monkey!

JOHN: Aagh! Let's go to the disco. You know, maybe you can't live in the now . . . When did you last get pissed? . . . you know, I've never seen you pissed . . . When did you last get a good laugh? I've not seen you laugh since I've been here.

VOYO: (Returning) Hello, guys . . . I walked up and down . . . nothing! I need a woman . . . Tonight I must fuck . . . Nice little chiquita . . . lovely! Maybe nice Mexican woman . . . Not go with prostitute . . . Yesterday with prostitute . . . She was nice . . . She made me bargain fifty dollars OK, but all night long . . . beautiful . . . So let's go eat something, my friend, something nice and hot . . . like enchiladas with chilli sauce . . . Good for you. Then nice girl . . . This one here in the lobby, I fuck her already . . . Nice . . . very nice . . . but it was not the best time of the month . . . Ahhh! The sheets . . . Chambermaid had to clean up . . . Oh, my God! Still, they're used to it . . . I take margarita, too! (Blackout.)

The next night.
WILL: So, I was there and didn't score with anything . . . It's over four weeks and I haven't even been out with a girl . . . I mean, just to sit in a restaurant and talk, you know, just talk. That would be good . . . rap a bit . . . sound off . . . have a drink . . . civilized . . . not like Voyo . . . 'I must have fuck . . . me have cock like horse prick.' The disco was poison. It's the worst place in the world with that jerk Mexicano pop shit. So I left. I couldn't take any more. You had to shout in that dump. I mean it's the lowest common denominator of human intelligence and I'm supposed to find life there . . . So I just walked down the street . . . It was hot like it always is . . . That hot air that wraps itself around you . . . and you can't sleep . . . And so I walked and this woman came up to me and said . . . you know . . . if I wanted to go with her. I said, 'How much?' And she said five thousand pesos. That is twenty-five dollars . . . What the fuck. I was dying for a woman. I mean I could have stuck it in a tree . . . You know, I was desperate for a good fuck . . . You know how it is . . . huh? I get pretty intense. You notice . . . So, OK. And she was British . . . one of your countrymen. Yeah, some hooker from England. Making a living in Acapulco. She was a fuckin' mess, right. But she was OK. Ain't that funny . . . Who do I meet in Acapulco but some English girl walking down a hot street at three in the morning? She had a tooth missing here. (Points.) So she came back but it was a terrible fuck . . . She was terrible but I enjoyed it. She just lay there like she was dead so I ploughed into her. I wanted a real dirty fuck and I just got on with it. It didn't matter any more . . . But what a slag . . . What a disgusting British hooker in Acapulco with a front tooth missing . . . And so I fucked her and she lay there . . . and like I was in a way glad for her to be there . . . just to have the company. She passed out . . . and I was going up the wall . . . I couldn't sleep . . . I kept

thinking about the one in the hotel . . . the cock-teaser . . . I'm sure she wanted me . . . I was going up the wall and this slag was sleeping in my nice clean bed and then she woke up and took a leak, and I put it in her mouth while she was taking a leak . . . Yeah! It's gross, and she flopped out again but I had to get up at six a.m. to go to work . . . It was a work day for me . . . I said, 'Come on. Get up . . . get out of here . . . I gotta work.' She was out to the world . . . I took her by the ears. I said, 'Look, you gotta get the fuck outa here!'

STEVE: No . . . by the ears?

WILL: Yeah . . . I swear it was the only thing I could get hold of that was showing above the sheets . . . I got hold of her ears . . . I said, 'I got to work!' So she got up and left with me and we split in the foyer so no one would see us together . . . but downstairs I see her queuing for crowd work! She was trying to get on the movie!

STEVE: You have to be careful . . .

WILL: Yeah . . . She was really a slag . . . So I went to the doc on the set . . . (Make mine a vino tinto, Roga) . . . What are you drinking?

STEVE: Margarita.

WILL: I said, 'Gimme a shot' . . . He said, 'Wait, give it a couple of days . . . and see . . . don't panic.'

STEVE: Be careful . . . You might get herpes . . .

WILL: I had it! It's psychological! It's a piece of shit . . . I had it and worried myself sick . . . I went to the doctors . . . You know how you know. You get these little blisters on your dick and the next day it becomes a sore and it hurts when you fuck . . . I had it but I beat it. Mind over matter . . . I was strong . . . Everybody makes a big deal over it like you got the plague. Everybody worries so much they keep bringing it back. They're always in stress . . . But I beat it. I was strong . . . I said, 'Fuck you' and it never once came back. It went away. Yeah . . . Oh, once it did come back after three months. Same thing. But I said to myself, 'I'm gonna fuck no matter what.' And it went away . . . When I worried it came back, but when I said, 'I'll fuck with it or without it' it

disappeared . . . And my woman who I was living with . . . not once did she catch it!
VOYO: Hello, guys . . . Oh, my God! Last night I didn't sleep.
WILL: What happened?
VOYO: Small one . . . little chiquita in the green top . . . she came back and stayed all night . . . I fuck like horse . . . huge horse prick . . . and do everything . . . (Mimes with tongue.) Oh my God! Beautiful! It's beautiful! It's what you need . . . Be free and enjoy . . . Good food and drink and the nice lady and (More tongue) that's life! You think Stallone can do that . . . Sure . . . he'd like . . . go to disco . . . find nice chiquita and (Mime) but he's trapped with those muscle men . . . But they are weak . . . not really strong at all . . . just puffed up . . . unnatural . . . I am natural . . . real strength . . . strength . . . I have real strength . . . When I was little I would run up mountains in Yugoslavia . . . I lifted huge barrels in my work . . . My legs are like tree trunks . . . Not from gym with weights and fagotty pop music for homosexuals who want to look beautiful . . . Weights not give you real power . . . In fight, I kill these bodybuilders . . . or karate experts . . . In street they are nothing . . . I say to stunt men . . . 'Hit me . . . Go on, hit me' . . . But they dare not . . . 'Punch me in the stomach' . . . But they frightened . . . I kill them . . . They know that!
JOHN: I'm exhausted . . . I didn't sleep a wink . . . I fucked all night . . . Those birds from the boutique.
VOYO: I fuck the little one in green . . . you know . . . She sweet . . . all night (Mime) prick like horse . . . Steve, what you do?
STEVE: I walked down the street . . . It was a hundred degrees out there . . . It must have been.
JOHN: It was fucking hot . . . I know that . . .
STEVE: The sea was brown from the hurricane . . . like it was full of shit and mud from the sewage overflow . . . Nobody swam in it . . . except me . . . Mexicans and their families . . . All the kids threw themselves into the sea . . . The mothers went in with their dresses on . . . The tourists stayed inside the hotel pool and ordered big fruity cocktails

and rubbed themselves with oil . . . They kept stroking themselves . . . First one and then the partner . . . And you could tell by the way they applied the oil how much they valued their flesh . . . Outside it was hotter than hell . . . But I walked for a while . . . Like thinking what to do . . . And I passed a mother and child . . . Like it was familiar . . . The outstretched arm . . . The baby in the other arm . . . sleeping . . . or just half-listless . . . And then the others . . . All the outstretched arms down the street . . . like branches . . . outstretched . . . and the gesture . . . putting their fingers to their mouth . . .

JOHN: Don't let them fool you, my friend . . . This is their way of life. To beg is not dishonourable to them . . . They feed off the tourists . . .

STEVE: Then I sat and had a coffee and saw eyes everywhere . . . Dark eyes following and watching me eat and then they'd come up . . . Like dogs begging for something or selling a little plate with pictures on it. So I bought a little plate and then another came up and then another . . . They came with their large brown eyes and outstretched hands . . . begging, cajoling, wheedling . . . trying to sell me chewing gum . . . They had these little boxes of chicklets . . . They tried to sell me a piece and the box was already looking old and broken . . . And the mother would be waiting at a distance . . . like she was pimping off the only thing she had . . . the eyes of her children . . . 'Cause the tourists couldn't resist . . . They were too much like little dolls . . . Maybe three or four years old . . . Little brown dolls. There was this smell everywhere . . . As I walked, I could smell it . . . Like the sewers had broken down . . . And nobody walked except the Mexicans and the shit smell grew stronger and then it subsided after a while, like the whole town was built on a great cake of shit and could only just process the amount it had and was on the breaking point. And then it was too hot, so I sat for a while and more kids came by like moths round a flame and the cats were so thin . . . they looked like Hollywood starlets . . . There were little stalls selling the dead bits of fish that you don't eat . . . like the slimy bits of offal that you would prefer not to think about . . . They were cooked and chopped up with onions and rolled into tortillas . . . Some shelled things that looked like sea lice were having their stomachs scraped out . . . They were wiggling like worms . . . little slug-like things . . . Two men were crouched over a bucket on a side street in a mass of shells and slime and flies . . . They were excavating these little shreds of flesh . . . And cats would leap in and out and eat the bits that fell . . . So this man I saw was selling corn on the cob. He was sitting on a little wooden box with his cobs . . . maybe a couple of dozen . . . He sat there all night . . . facing the street so all of the exhaust pipes from the buses belched all over him and he waited and waited . . . and this was his life forever.

JOHN: You're romanticizing . . . He enjoys his life . . . He has his friends and community . . . Don't project your Western life style on him . . . He's happy!

STEVE: His 'life' . . . his actual world was the couple of dozen of pieces of worn-out corn that are kept hot on his little stove . . . That was his life . . . And I walked past and I saw the wooden box and the smaller box for the corn and he had laid it out to be attractive . . . He laid out the corns like they were gold and in the corner of the box was a sauce for the corn and they were sixty pesos . . . That's thirty cents . . . And if he sold them all he'd make three dollars fifty . . . But he would have to sit there maybe for seven hours . . . That's fifty cents per hour. And then he would have to be lucky . . . So he sits there night after night with his world which is the corns that nobody really wants . . .

JOHN: It's probably pin money for him . . . He's got a job somewhere during the day, my friend. It's probably a way of making a few pesos . . . He's happy like that. He's happier than you . . .

STEVE: So this is what Cortés brought to the Indians . . . Is this the great civilization Spain brought to Mexico? This is the fruit of Christian civilization? The Aztecs were murdered by the Spanish . . . their temples destroyed and their race corrupted and for what . . . So that an Indian can stand outside the Acapulco Plaza Hotel . . . all day long . . . in the heat . . . just in the hope that a bored tourist might . . . if he is lucky, the Indian, that is . . . very lucky . . . might, in a moment's frivolous desire . . . with that greed that all tourists have . . . that desire to consume . . . no matter what . . . just something to fill a space . . . might buy something from him . . . that thing being an elephant badly carved out of a piece of onyx . . . so he might if he is lucky . . . sell it to a tourist who, to digest his breakfast, feels amused to bargain and play a little game . . . and he and many others will wait in the heat all day long . . . and not sell anything at all . . . but if he does . . . his meaning of life will have been fulfilled . . . But he won't sell it because there are hundreds and hundreds outside these charnel houses like the Acapulco Plaza Hotel . . . So when he wakes up in the morning his hope and future lie in that little elephant. So Spain well and truly screwed Mexico . . . for centuries.

VOYO: That must have been a great fuck!
JOHN: Oh, come on . . . You're talking history . . . *La quenta por favor* . . . I'll get it . . . How much?
BARMAN: You had six margaritas . . . That's twelve bucks. Thank you, my friend!
(Blackout.)

JOHN: It was the last day . . . At last we were getting out of the cage. We'd been in there for four weeks and we were being rescued. Heyyy! Well, ten years, according to the script . . . So Stallone comes over and springs us . . . 'Come on,' he said . . . 'Come on out of there!' So we dash out . . . But we haven't been out of the cage in ten years.
WILL: No, fifteen . . . He said fifteen!
JOHN: Fifteen years we'd been in that cage . . . Maybe fifteen years and you'd stumble out . . . Right? You'd fall out . . . You'd crawl out . . . but we had to dash out and run . . . Run?!! We couldn't walk after fifteen years . . . We'd hobble, we'd crawl . . . we'd be feeble and frightened. 'Hey, what's going on?' . . . All confused. Maybe we'd even try to go back to the cage . . . You know . . . It's been fifteen fucking years, man. One guy would run back . . . Yeah, to

the cage . . . Maybe that's his home . . . The cage is what he *knew! At least he knew there he was safe!* But no, we'd dash out like we were rushing to get dinner at the Acapulco Plaza . . .

WILL: I saw the explosion . . . They were blowing up the camp . . . We were being saved . . . It was amazing!

JOHN: But the First Assistant . . . the Englishman . . . said, 'Come out of the cage like you were leaving a Glasgow pub on a Saturday night . . .' That was perfect . . . That was the image we needed!

WILL: The blast of the explosion was deafening . . . We were being saved . . . What would we do in that situation? . . . The director said, 'Do something . . . You're being saved . . . You're happy . . . You're crazy . . . You're getting out!!' I tell you, it was great . . . We were working at last.

JOHN: Not just background . . . Not just scenography . . .

WILL: No, we were actors . . . We had to do something . . . I hugged the prisoners . . . I hugged and kissed them . . . There were tears in my eyes . . . I was screaming . . . I put my hands through the bars like this . . . I put my fist through and shook it at the bastards . . . It felt great! I was happy . . . I was hugging and crying and then that idiot . . . That other idiot in the cage had to copy me. He put his fist through the bars and did the same as me, the squirt . . . The fire was everywhere . . . The blaze was amazing . . . You felt it going through you and the cameras were on us the whole time . . . You *had* to do something . . . Then Stallone came to get us out . . .

JOHN: 'Come on out of there!' He came up . . . big machine-gun . . . like a great phallus . . .

WILL: He looked at me . . . For a moment he looked me in the eye . . . There he was . . . sweat band round his forehead . . . muscles and veins bulging out . . . gripping a huge black machine-gun . . . an M-60 . . . like a god . . . He looked like the angel of death . . . sweat pouring out . . . muscles all flexed for action . . . This M-60 like a huge cock . . . You're right . . . He looked me in the eye like he knew me . . . like he actually felt I was all right and he said, 'Come on . . . Come on . . . Let's go!' And we jumped or crawled out of the cage . . . And he put his hand on my shoulder . . . And it felt good . . . Like he was acknowledging what I had done . . . Maybe he touched the other prisoners as they came out . . . I didn't see. But he touched me and I felt like a god was touching me and it felt great . . . You see, 'cause I was in that stinkin' cage for years. I was in that shit and filth and along comes this guy, hair flying and built like he was carved out of rock, and takes me away from all that . . . And we did the shot again and again and he touched me on the shoulder each time, like it wasn't just an accident the first time . . . as if we had some kind of unspoken communication . . . I worked . . . I felt great . . . I'm high now . . . I'm high from it . . . It's good to work . . . You know what I'm saying . . .

VOYO: Great! I like to act . . . I wanna act the big parts . . . Spartacus . . . Odysseus . . . Zorba . . . Strong men. There's no strong men any more. They are nothing . . . just puffed up in expensive gyms in Hollywood . . . They are nothing . . . faggots . . . cock-suckers . . . all puffed up . . . that Schwarzenegger, he have no strength . . . He is nothing . . . Not real power . . . He frightened of me . . . If I went to him and say, 'Fight' he would turn away . . . There used to be strong men . . . Anthony Quinn . . . John Wayne . . . Like a piece of mountain . . . Marlon Brando . . . You believed them . . . Now, they are nothing . . . In this film, I must pretend to be weak . . . How can Stallone kill me? . . . How? I kill him . . . I am much stronger than he . . .

JOHN: It's supposed to be acting.

VOYO: Yeah, I know . . . But the audience has got to believe . . . He cannot beat me with fist . . . If he hit me on the head with hammer I just stand there . . . It must look real . . . People aren't stupid . . . Wad you think? . . . The American people all stupid idiots? . . . They laugh . . . He goes, 'boom! boom!' And I supposed to collapse . . . They laugh . . . No, he must use trick . . . Like Odysseus . . . He use brains and escapes under sheep . . . So Stallone must use trick 'cause he cannot beat me with fist . . . It's stupid . . . I'm like giant!

JOHN: Kirk Douglas!

VOYO: Right . . . Kirk Douglas!

JOHN: They could act!

VOYO: Oh, my friend!

JOHN: Rod Steiger . . . When he comes on the set, the whole place lights up . . . He just comes on . . . First take perfect . . . Two takes and that's enough . . . He says . . . 'That's enough!'

WILL: The scene in the cab . . . *On the Waterfront* . . . He played the older brother . . .

JOHN: *Napoleon!!*

WILL: *The Illustrated Man!*

JOHN: *Across the Bridge* . . . Shot that in Mexico.

WILL: He's a great actor . . .

JOHN: *The Pawnbroker* . . .

WILL: 'Charlie . . . I could have been somebody . . . I coulda had class.' Great acting . . . You know what I'm saying . . . I'd love to act . . . You know I'd love to act with you . . . I mean act on the stage . . . I'm dying to act . . . I'd go anywhere . . . Well, get a little theatre off-Broadway . . . There are dozens of little theatres . . . Cost you peanuts . . . You do a deal . . . We'll act something . . . I did a play in L.A. The Pilot Theater . . . You know it! Oh, sure, you did a play there once . . . It was great . . . Great space . . . Lots of space to move in . . . I came out every night and I felt purged . . . renewed . . . like you put your guts out there each night and when you put it back, it feels . . . great! I was flying . . . I was alive . . . You'd get in . . . The day was just an interlude before the night . . . Your stomach would twist up like a coiled spring but then you'd unwind it and let it out . . . There's nothing like it . . . I loved it . . . I'd work for nothing . . . Naturally, I gotta earn a living . . . But we start with nothing . . . just a beating heart . . . and a bit of spit . . . What else: . . Shmocks only work for money . . . A warrior works for life! He'll work for nothing if it touches him on the soul

. . . Pay the rent . . . that's all I ask . . . We all work together, huh?
VOYO: Spartacus, Odysseus, Zorba, Dostoyevsky!
WILL: Hey, Steve . . . You say you write . . . Why not write a play about *us*!
(Blackout.)

STEVE: I woke up . . . It was still dark . . . Like I was waking with the beat of others . . . Thousands of miles away . . . I lay in thought and was not here . . . I haven't been here since I've been here . . . I've been here only in the body but my mind has been trapped . . . It's been borrowed from time to time . . . Otherwise, it's been in a cold, dreary country . . . like it was pulled back into the fog . . . I awoke in the sun . . . I was like Frankenstein's monster . . . all there except for something missing . . . Like a soul that couldn't catch up with the body as the body flew through space . . . The wrench pulled it away . . . like you pull the skin away from a fruit . . . I was there except in soul, so I watched the souls of others . . . I watched and observed them from my body . . . like I was secretly stealing bits of them to make up one of my own . . . I watched their passions and frustrations . . . their needs and joys so easily spilling out. I watched them and heard them but I was in a block of ice . . . Their breath warmed me and made cracks in it sometimes . . . So I borrowed bits of their souls and wrote it down to give me one that I could use or borrow . . . I was caged and my soul was in flight . . . not daring or wishing to share the cage where I chose to live. I awoke and it was dark . . . The dawn was just edging the darkness away and the sea was pounding against the shore . . . I heard the beating of my heart . . . I lay in a large bed without a soul to comfort me . . . I awoke like I was keeping time with another land . . . The bed was large and empty and there were drinks in the fridge which were replenished daily . . . The fishing nets were out and it was still dark . . . He was thrilled to be sitting in a cage . . . so excited . . . 'Stallone touched me!' The dawn sent long snake-like fingers of light and the day oozed slowly on to

Acapulco beach . . . Scuba diving or a one-day trip around the city . . . The stretch of beach was lined with huge hotels like ancient temples where you came to make your sacrificial offerings . . . They lay around the pool like white slugs . . . At four p.m. is volleyball in the pool . . .
(Blackout.)

JOHN: I know the Mexicans . . . They can't be bought . . . They'll give you anything and they'll take your money but they can't be bought . . . They'll say, 'Fuck off, gringo!' They want respect . . . That's important to a Mexican . . . There are lots of Mexicans on this film and you notice they're all good workers . . . But they must have respect . . . This film's costing twenty-eight million dollars . . . That's the budget . . . Twenty-eight. It's no secret . . . I even read it in the *Acapulco News* . . . And do you know what he's getting? Six million dollars . . . or even eight million.

WILL: No . . . he's getting maybe four million dollars up front . . .

JOHN: All right, so he's only getting four million dollars. So he must have made millions already . . .

WILL: Maybe another ten million dollars from the 'Rocky' movies . . .

JOHN: All that money . . . But he invests it and makes more money and that creates labour, doesn't it? I'm doing all right . . . I'm making five hundred dollars a week, plus my *per diem*, and I'm saving money. I'm actually saving. Listen. It's like a fortune that has no meaning. If it's three million dollars, it may as well be four . . . And it's cheap to shoot in Mexico so you can save another few million . . . They get nothing here since inflation . . . You know how much a labourer gets? My friend, do you know? . . . To build one of those condominiums . . . five dollars a day . . . He'll be happy to shift cement for five dollars per day . . . 'Cause that's all he gets paid . . . So you can buy places cheap here . . . That's why they all pour into Mexico. An apartment overlooking the sea, you'll get for twenty thousand dollars or a palace for forty thousand and a couple of Peons thrown in

as staff . . . They'll do it for nothing. They come with the apartment to clean up . . . do your cooking . . . They're happy to do it.
STEVE: Like slaves . . . Better the master they know . . .
JOHN: No! It's in your mind they're slaves . . . They want to work for you . . . They're proud . . . They want to show you how good they can be . . . They don't *need* like you or the Western gringo . . . Don't project your needs on to them . . . They're happy to show you their skills . . .
WILL: Yeah . . . Like that party on Sunday . . . you took us to . . . given by those rich white Mexicans . . . where they wanted really a few actors from the set . . . and the slaves were skulking round the kitchen while the important slugs made the small chat round the pool . . . while the monkeys made their idiot chat and talked money and the biggest pile of bullshit I ever heard . . . the Mexicans are sitting in the shadows preparing the food . . .
JOHN: They are happy, my friend . . . They are happier cooking in the kitchen and taking pride in the food than making the small chat with the idiots outside . . . You're right . . .
WILL: I was there . . . They talked shit from beginning to end . . . I couldn't hear it any more . . . I felt sick . . . Then they had a game of throwing each other in the pool. Hah! Hah! Hah! Why is it that so many people with money act like assholes?
JOHN: I know a few without money who do, too!
WILL: There was a couple of the slugs from the hotel. The evil chicks who hang around all day doing nothing and we were served this delicious lunch which was like in their image . . . It was a whole pig with a fat tomato in its mouth . . . And nobody said anything . . . They sat around like they were verbally sterile . . . impotent . . . 'What are you doing?' 'I'm just getting pissed.' 'I manage condominiums . . .' Who gives a shit? 'Hey, isn't this nice?' 'Isn't this beautiful?' 'Hey, what a beautiful house.' It was a sewer 'cause it processed shit. I had to leave, John . . . I mean, you were wonderful . . . You are an expert shit-talker to idiots . . . I admire you for it . . . You're the court jester who ends up

screwing them . . . And their faces were so ugly . . . Tell me, why are the very rich so very ugly? . . . The Indian Peons are beautiful . . . slim and agile and if you had a choice of what to be . . . a rich and ugly white, or a poor and beautiful Indian, I know what I should be . . . 'Cause you can always get rich or *maybe* you can . . . but if you are a fat ugly self-centred greasy white bastard, it's very difficult to be beautiful . . . Am I right?

STEVE: Cortés, the great Spanish conqueror, surrounded Mexico and starved them out and then he burned it to the ground . . . Montezuma, the Aztec king, waited in his palace, listening to the messengers tell him news of the strange white men who were half horse and half man. They had never seen a horse before . . . They must be gods, they thought . . . So Cortés came and stole the gold and the treasures of the Aztecs and then he destroyed Mexico, which was the most beautiful city in the world . . . But he gave them Christianity . . . They raped their Indian women and melted down their great works of art, but they gave them Christianity . . . You cannot conquer any other way . . . If you leave a people with their religion, you leave them with the spark that will one day become a raging fire . . . And he told them about Christ and that Christ was a man and Mary his mother and God his father and the Aztecs were confused by three gods, when Cortés said there was only one . . . Then they were told about eating Christ in a biscuit and drinking his blood and the Aztecs said, 'We, too, eat the flesh of our enemies.' But they were punished by the Spaniards for doing such terrible things . . . Then they were confused by worshipping two sticks and three gods but in time . . . Now, there came poverty and disease where before there was none. The Aztecs had built highways and along the highways there were toilets . . . Yes, believe it or not, there were toilets and the waste was used as fertilizer and so everything had a value . . . The Spanish brought little glass beads and exchanged them for gold by tricking the Indians into believing they were precious stones. But the gold was not enough . . . Spain wanted to own the whole place and so cut down the Indian

... The Indians wandered around confused. They had lost their city and their gods, and were offered instead two sticks to worship since they could not yet understand the new gods ... But out of the ashes of the past a new temple arose to celebrate the re-creation of Mexico ... The Acapulco Plaza Hotel.

BARMAN: I gotta close the bar ... *Esta mañana* ... Gentlemen.
STEVE: So you finish next week?
JOHN: Yeah! I think so ... We're out of the cage now ... We're doing the chopper scene.
STEVE: That's a relief, eh?
JOHN: You can't imagine what it's like ... five of us in the cage ...
STEVE: So, you're free.
JOHN: Yeeeeh ...
STEVE: What you gonna do?
JOHN: I'll head back for Mexico City ... I've got this office there I was telling you about and there's been a lot of work coming in ... You know I make commercials ... Sure, for Mexican TV, but since the peso was devalued it caught us all with our pants down.
STEVE: What will you do?
WILL: I dunno. Maybe I'll go back to Mexico City ... It was always good for me ... I had this instinct to come ... I can always escape to Mexico. I got married here, you know ... We stayed at this amazing place near Oaxaca ('*Owuka*') on the beach ... Nothing ... Just nothing ... Only the Indians and you could hear wild animals at night ... When I need to escape, I always come here ... It's real ... You know what I mean ... I live in a small hotel in the Pink Zone ... It's called Hotel Angelo ... Five dollars a night ... But I'm thinking of going to Paris to see Polanski ...
STEVE: How will you do that?
WILL: Just go up to him ... He's a man ... He knows ... Just say, 'I want to work for you ... I've come six thousand miles ... I'd be a good pirate' ... He's doing a movie on pirates ... He needs someone like me ... 'Use me, Roman!' I'll find him ... Shit! I won't go to a casting

director. I'll find *him*! I hear he's a good guy . . . I'd be good in his film, in the galleys . . . Hey, don't you think I'd be a good pirate?

STEVE: Sure, why not? . . .

Selected Grove Press Paperbacks

62480-7	ACKER, KATHY / Great Expectations: A Novel / $6.95
17458-5	ALLEN, DONALD & BUTTERICK, GEORGE F., eds. / The Postmoderns: The New American Poetry Revised / $9.95
17397-X	ANONYMOUS / My Secret Life / $4.95
62433-5	BARASH, D. and LIPTON, J. / Stop Nuclear War! A Handbook / $7.95
17087-3	BARNES, JOHN / Evita—First Lady: A Biography of Eva Peron / $4.95
17208-6	BECKETT, SAMUEL / Endgame / $3.50
17299-X	BECKETT, SAMUEL / Three Novels: Molloy, Malone Dies and The Unnamable / $6.95
17204-3	BECKETT, SAMUEL / Waiting for Godot / $3.95
62064-X	BECKETT, SAMUEL / Worstward Ho / $5.95
17244-2	BORGES, JORGE LUIS / Ficciones / $6.95
17112-8	BRECHT, BERTOLT / Galileo / $3.95
17106-3	BRECHT, BERTOLT / Mother Courage and Her Children / $2.95
17393-7	BRETON ANDRE / Nadja / $6.95
17439-9	BULGAKOV, MIKHAIL / The Master and Margarita / $5.95
17108-X	BURROUGHS, WILLIAM S. / Naked Lunch / $4.95
17749-5	BURROUGHS, WILLIAM S. / The Soft Machine, Nova Express, The Wild Boys: Three Novels / $5.95
62488-2	CLARK, AL, ed. / The Film Year Book 1984 / $12.95
17535-2	COWARD, NOEL / Three Plays (Private Lives, Hay Fever, Blithe Spirit) / $7.95
17219-1	CUMMINGS, E.E. / 100 Selected Poems / $3.95
17327-9	FANON, FRANZ / The Wretched of the Earth / $4.95
17483-6	FROMM, ERICH / The Forgotten Language / $6.95
17390-2	GENET, JEAN / The Maids and Deathwatch: Two Plays / $8.95
17838-6	GENET, JEAN / Querelle / $4.95
17662-6	GERVASI, TOM / Arsenal of Democracy II / $12.95
17956-0	GETTLEMAN, MARVIN, et.al. eds. / El Salvador: Central America in the New Cold War / $9.95
17648-0	GIRODIAS, MAURICE, ed. / The Olympia Reader / $5.95
62490-4	GUITAR PLAYER MAGAZINE / The Guitar Player Book (Revised and Updated Edition) $11.95
62003-8	HITLER, ADOLF / Hitler's Secret Book / $7.95
17125-X	HOCHHUTH, ROLF / The Deputy / $7.95
62115-8	HOLMES, BURTON / The Olympian Games in Athens, 1896 / $6.95

17209-4	IONESCO, EUGENE / Four Plays (The Bald Soprano, The Lesson, The Chairs, and Jack or The Submission) / $6.95
17226-4	IONESCO, EUGENE / Rhinoceros / $5.95
62123-9	JOHNSON, CHARLES / Oxherding Tale / $6.95
17254-X	KEENE, DONALD, ed. / Modern Japanese Literature / $12.50
17952-8	KEROUAC, JACK / The Subterraneans / $3.50
62424-6	LAWRENCE, D.H. / Lady Chatterley's Lover / $3.95
17016-4	MAMET, DAVID / American Buffalo / $4.95
17760-6	MILLER, HENRY / Tropic of Cancer / $4.95
17295-7	MILLER, HENRY / Tropic of Capricorn / $3.95
17869-6	NERUDA, PABLO / Five Decades: Poems 1925-1970. Bilingual ed. / $12.50
17092-X	ODETS, CLIFFORD / Six Plays (Waiting for Lefty, Awake and Sing, Golden Boy, Rocket to the Moon, Till the Day I Die, Paradise Lost) / $7.95
17650-2	OE, KENZABURO / A Personal Matter / $6.95
17232-9	PINTER, HAROLD / The Birthday Party & The Room / $6.95
17251-5	PINTER, HAROLD / The Homecoming / $5.95
17539-5	POMERANCE, BERNARD / The Elephant Man / $5.95
17827-0	RAHULA, WALPOLA / What the Buddha Taught / $6.95
17658-8	REAGE, PAULINE / The Story of O, Part II; Return to the Chateau / $3.95
62169-7	RECHY, JOHN / City of Night / $4.50
62001-1	ROSSET, BARNEY and JORDAN, FRED, eds. / Evergreen Review No. 98 / $5.95
62498-X	ROSSET, PETER and VANDERMEER, JOHN / The Nicaragua Reader / $9.95
17119-5	SADE, MARQUIS DE / The 120 Days of Sodom and Other Writings / $12.50
62009-7	SEGALL, J. PETER / Deduct This Book: How Not to Pay Taxes While Ronald Reagan is President / $6.95
17467-4	SELBY, HUBERT / Last Exit to Brooklyn / $3.95
17948-X	SHAWN, WALLACE, and GREGORY, ANDRE / My Dinner with Andre / $6.95
17797-5	SNOW, EDGAR / Red Star Over China / $9.95
17260-4	STOPPARD, TOM / Rosencrantz and Guildenstern Are Dead / $3.95
17474-7	SUZUKI, D.T. / Introduction to Zen Buddhism / $3.95
17599-9	THELWELL, MICHAEL / The Harder They Come: A Novel about Jamaica / $7.95
17969-2	TOOLE, JOHN KENNEDY / A Confederacy of Dunces / $4.50
17418-6	WATTS, ALAN W. / The Spirit of Zen / $3.95

GROVE PRESS, INC., 920 Broadway, New York, N.Y. 10010